# SAFE PLACE

# SAFE PLACE

## Guidelines for Creating an Abuse-Free Environment

### EDITOR

Rev. Marv Parker

### CONTRIBUTORS

Burt Manchester, Brenda Philips and Jonathan Youngman

**CHRISTIAN PUBLICATIONS, INC.**
CAMP HILL, PENNSYLVANIA

**CHRISTIAN PUBLICATIONS, INC.**

3825 Hartzdale Drive, Camp Hill, PA 17011

www.christianpublications.com

*Faithful, biblical publishing since 1883*

ISBN: 0-87509-979-3

© 2002 by the Disciplemaking Ministries Office
of Christian Publications, Inc.

Cover design by Rick Hemphill

NOTE: Italicized words in Scripture quotations are the emphasis of the author.

Disciplemaking Ministries Office
Christian Publications, Inc.
3825 Hartzdale Drive
Camp Hill, PA 17011
www.christianpublications.com
1.800.233.4443

# CONTENTS

The issue of physical and sexual abuse seems completely out of context for the church setting and the ministry environment. Sadly, however, the church has not been exempt from such concerns. In fact, the abuse issue has become a major concern in our society—one that church leaders *must not* ignore. The church and its leaders should be singularly proactive in taking steps and establishing procedures to avoid such situations. (Please note: Throughout this book the term "church" refers to both the local church and to other ministry organizations.)

*Safe Place* is designed to assist leaders of local churches in creating policies for *safe people* to minister in *safe places* through *safe programs*. By creating and following these policies, the church will be able to relax as it pursues its God-given mission of making healthy disciples of children, youth and adults. The primary purpose of *Safe Place* is to safeguard both students and leaders in the church setting.

Understanding that true ministry cannot take place when the care and welfare of students are not first addressed, *Safe Place* provides guidelines for church leaders that will enable them to establish a plan that will provide a hedge of safety for both their students and their volunteer leaders. While such safeguards do not provide a 100 percent guarantee that accidents or abuse will not happen, they will greatly reduce the risk of such occurrences.

**The purpose of this manual is not to give legal counsel or advice.** However, it is imperative that local church leaders do everything possible to provide a safe and secure ministry environment for every individual, at every age level—both students and volunteers. Since state and local requirements vary, it is important that legal advice and competent professional assistance be sought as you adapt a "safe place" policy for your church.

*Safe Place* is *not* intended to be "one-size-fits-all." Rather, it is a resource of information—information that will assist leaders in developing clear policies and procedures that will promote a safe and secure ministry environment.

To make this resource as practical and useful as possible the following features have been added:

- *Training Points* are identified throughout the manual with the symbol seen at left. They are essential items which must be communicated to volunteer leaders, teach-

1

ers and workers. They form the basis of the reproducible "Points to Ponder" worksheets found in chapter 8. The worksheets can also be found on the CD which is located inside the back cover of this book.

- *Training Tips* are provided throughout the manual. They may be found in the highlighted areas of each chapter. Each "Training Tips" section provides leaders with ideas to help communicate content in fun, interactive ways.

- All *forms and charts* in the appendix section are available on the CD located inside the back cover of this book.

- All *forms and charts* provided may be personalized and reproduced for ministry purposes, but not for resale. Feel free to make as many copies as needed to meet the needs of your church.

May God grant you the wisdom and insight necessary to develop the policies and procedures essential to making your church a safe place.

## TRAINING TIPS

### PRE-SESSION ICE BREAKER IDEA #1: LET'S TALK SAFEGUARDS!

Divide class into groups of three to five individuals. Assign one of the following topics to each group: 1) sports (football, baseball, basketball, etc.); 2) travel (auto, bus, plane, etc.); 3) workplace (factory, office, warehouse, etc.); or 4) home (kitchen, garage, shop, yard, etc.). Have each group identify and list safety issues that need to be addressed to ensure a safe environment. After five minutes have a group member report his or her findings to the class. Answers may include: 1) sports: proper equipment, field, court or surface, body protection, etc.; 2) travel: airline security, seat belts, speed limits, etc.; 3) workplace: proper equipment, breaks, warning signs, etc.; 4) home: cleaning fluids out of reach, power tool guards, lock guards to keep preschoolers out of cabinets, etc. Explain that just as there are essential safeguards in place for such activities and locations, policies and procedures must be implemented to ensure a "safe place" in church ministry.

### PRE-SESSION ICE BREAKER IDEA #2: SAFE PLACE ACROSTIC

Using the letters of "Safe Place" and the characteristics of a safe place, create an acrostic. (Example: <u>S</u>–secure, <u>A</u>–age appropriate, <u>F</u>–fun, <u>E</u>–efficient . . . <u>P</u> . . . .)

W henever a policy or plan of this magnitude comes to one's attention, it is all too easy to set it aside and say "This is too much," "This is too overwhelming" or "Where do I begin?" Despite the daunting nature of such an undertaking, and in light of the need and the pain it could save, it is strongly recommended that you seriously consider this manual and the establishment of a "Safe Place Plan" for your church.

While it will take some time to develop your plan and fully integrate it into actual practice, the key is to begin right away. The following "action steps" have been provided to help you work through the process.

Step #1: Become thoroughly familiar with the content of this book.

Step #2: Present a brief overview of *Safe Place* to your key leaders, emphasizing the need to develop a Safe Place Plan.

Step #3: Establish a small committee to develop a Safe Place Plan.

Step #4: Present the proposed Safe Place Plan to leadership for approval.

Step #5: Educate and train all leaders, teachers and workers about the new Safe Place Plan. (Remember: "Training Points" and "Training Tips" are provided throughout this book for training purposes. "Points to Ponder" worksheets with Leader's Guides are provided in Chapter 8 and on the enclosed CD.)

Step #6: Inform your constituency that a Safe Place Plan has been implemented.

Step #7: Monitor use of the Safe Place Plan and modify as needed.

# one

# UNDERSTANDING THE ISSUES

## A. UNDERSTANDING THE NEED

Church leaders are responsible for providing a safe and secure environment for their ministries. This responsibility includes recruiting and training volunteers, providing proper supervision, maintaining a safe facility and caring for the specific needs of individuals at every age level—children, youth and adult. One of the most vital needs in creating a safe place is to safeguard against child abuse. (Please note: Throughout this book the term "child" refers to individuals from birth to legal adult age.) The following quotes will highlight the need to take this issue seriously.

The following is an actual example of a situation that a church may face:

> . . . in Alaska . . . a church was found liable for in excess of one million dollars as a result of a nursery teacher abusing a young child. The court found that the church had been negligent in not doing a background check or reference review on the worker and it also failed to inquire of the worker on the application form if the worker had been a victim of abuse as a child, given the statistical inference that once a victim, such a person is more likely to be an abuser.[1]

While the issue of physical and sexual abuse is not a new topic, it is rapidly becoming the number one concern for organizations responsible for the care and safety of children. Almost every day we are confronted by stories in the media relating instances to actual and alleged abuse against children while in the care of boys' and girls' organizations, sports associations, day cares, schools, camps, churches and other charitable organizations such as orphanages, shelters and group homes. Apart from the obvious emotional and physical damage caused by such acts, many organizations are now facing the staggering financial costs resulting from civil liability judgments awarded to injured parties who are able to establish negligence against organizations due to the criminal actions of their employees or volunteers. One positive result of these highly publicized liability awards has been to heighten awareness on the part of organizations to take proactive measures to reduce the risk of abuse to children in their care, including the proper screening, training and supervision of those individuals working with children and young people.[2]

Consider the following realities that are true of our society today:

- "According to state Child Protective Services (CPS) agencies, more than 1 million children are victims of abuse and neglect each year."[3]
- One in three girls and one in five boys will be abused by the age of eighteen[4]
- Every ten minutes, five children are molested = one every two to three minutes[5]
- Top five reasons churches may be sued:
  - Negligence in screening and training workers
  - Negligence in event planning
  - Negligence in energy action
  - Negligence in supervision
  - Negligence in communication[6]

One survey showed that, by the age of eighteen, thirty-eight percent of women had been sexually abused by an adult or family member.[7]

TRAINING TIPS

- Share the above examples and/or others with which you are familiar.
- Collect local and national news items to validate the need for establishing a safe environment.
- Share above-mentioned stats or others that you can document to point out the need for the church to take the appropriate steps.

Local church leaders have a spiritual, moral and legal obligation to provide a safe and secure environment for all individuals—children, youth and adults—participating in church ministries. The emotional, physical and spiritual trauma to victims, the destructive consequences for abusers and the devastating effects on the credibility of the name of Christ and church ministry make it essential that the church take the appropriate steps to create a safe and secure environment and to assist in the prevention of abuse.

## B. UNDERSTANDING CHILD ABUSE

The specific definition of child abuse will vary from state to state. To find out the definitions and age guidelines for your state, contact your Department of Health and Human Services or your local law enforcement agencies.

Some general definitions are:

1. Child abuse is defined as a nonaccidental physical or mental injury or mistreatment caused by the acts or omissions of the child's parents or caretakers.

2. Abuse is categorized as physical, emotional, verbal or sexual.
   a. Physical abuse is nonaccidental injury of a child.
   b. Emotional abuse is chronic attitudes or acts that are likely to produce serious, long-term emotional disorders.
   c. Verbal abuse is communication by words (i.e., derogatory name calling, criticism, yelling), vocal tones and accompanying body language and attitudes which demean a person's appearance or worth.
   d. Sexual abuse is sexual exploitation of a child, consensual or not, for the sexual gratification of the perpetrator or a third party. Some sexual offenses are fondling; oral, genital or anal penetration; intercourse; forcible rape; exhibitionism; allowing children to witness sexual activity.

3. Neglect means failure of those responsible for the care of a child to meet the physical and emotional needs of the child to an extent that the child's health, development or safety are endangered.
   a. Physical neglect means failure to meet the basic requirements for supervision, housing, clothing, medical attention and nutrition.
   b. Emotional neglect means failure to provide the praise, love, nurturing and security essential to the psychological and social development of a child.

4. Adults, Elderly and People with Disabilities
   It is important for churches to recognize that many of the issues raised in the preceding definitions about child abuse can also be relevant to instances of abuse between adults and people with disabilities, or even between consenting adults. Even if

individuals involved may be consenting, issues of abuse might be raised because of the position of power one is vested with when serving as a spiritual/ministerial leader (i.e., adult Sunday school teacher, small group leader, counselor, etc.).

## C. Understanding the Church's Responsibility

1. The Scriptural and Moral Responsibility of Local Churches

   The Church represents Jesus Christ and must demonstrate and model His love, concern and holiness of life to everyone.

   The Scriptures say:

   a. "Avoid every kind of evil" (1 Thessalonians 5:22).

   b. "But among you there must not be even a hint of sexual immorality . . . because these are improper for God's holy people" (Ephesians 5:3).

   c. "But whoever causes one of these little ones who believe in Me to stumble, it would be better for him to have a heavy millstone hung around his neck, and to be drowned in the depth of the sea" (Matthew 18:6, NASB).

   d. "Brothers, if someone is caught in a sin, you who are spiritual should restore him gently. . . . Carry each other's burdens, and in this way you will fulfill the law of Christ" (Galatians 6:1-2).

   e. "Let the little children come to me, and do not hinder them, for the kingdom of heaven belongs to such as these" (Matthew 19:14).

   f. "Not many of you should presume to be teachers, my brothers, because you know that we who teach will be judged more strictly" (James 3:1).

   g. "Remember your leaders, who spoke the word of God to you. Consider the outcome of their way of life and imitate their faith" (Hebrews 13:7).

TRAINING TIP

• Print and hand out a selection of the above Scripture references to individuals as they arrive to class. Have them prepare to read them when called for during training session.

The guidelines presented in this book are set forth to provide a safe and nurturing environment in which we can bring individuals to the Savior. We view ourselves as partners with parents, seeking to provide quality care and instruction in our ministry to the family. All of the guidelines are designed to protect both student and volunteer and to promote spiritual growth, building healthy disciples at every age level.

Leaders are strongly encouraged to adopt these guidelines and procedures under the counsel of their legal advisor. Organizations may develop additional guidelines that are appropriate to their ministry settings and in keeping with the laws of their state.

Leadership should review and adopt established guidelines—a "Safe Place Plan"—as official church policy.

2. The Civil and Legal Liability of the Church

Increasingly, and often more dramatically, churches and their personnel (i.e., staff, directors, officers and ministers) are being held accountable for the acts of individual abusers within the church. The church and its leaders are held accountable even though neither were aware of the abuse or condoned it. Churches are being sued in civil courts for damages sustained by victims and their families. Those victims and their families are attempting to hold churches accountable by alleging that:

a. The church is vicariously liable for the acts of its personnel, be they paid staff or volunteer staff, regardless of whether the church itself was negligent or even knew of the abuse.

b. The church was negligent in hiring or accepting personnel, whether paid or volunteer.

c. The church was negligent in supervising or monitoring its personnel or membership.

It is perhaps, if one is cynical, the pressure of being found liable to compensate victims of abuse along with the corresponding fear of embarrassment, that has caused churches to respond to the issue of child abuse more than it is a newfound desire to otherwise address an age-old problem. Whatever the reason, it is timely for churches to now respond.[8]

Organizations operating in good faith and providing valuable services to the community are being held to a higher standard of accountability in this area, even to the point of being "guarantors" of conduct of volunteer employees.[9]

How would you respond if your church was involved in an abuse case and a lawyer asked the leadership of your church, "What did you do to prevent this tragedy from happening?" Your answer could be a deciding factor in whether or not the church is declared negligent.

# "What did you do to prevent this tragedy from happening?"

It should be noted that many insurance carriers exclude child molestation in their coverage, or if it is covered, the amounts for damages are far below what may be awarded by a court. Leaders are strongly encouraged to check with their insurance provider to ensure adequate coverage.

## ENDNOTES

1. Canadian Council of Christian Charities Bulletin #2, 1995, p. 5.
2. Canadian Council of Christian Charities Bulletin #2, 1997, p. 3.
3. Prevention Fundamentals, National Clearinghouse on Child Abuse and Neglect. Information updated on April 6, 2001, by webmaster_nccanch@calib.com.
4. Libby Leinweber, presenter, "Treating Adult and Child Survivors of Sexual Abuse and Trauma" seminar, Tucson, AZ. Carondelet Management Institute, Columbus, Ohio, July 12, 2000.
5. Dr. Robert J. Choun and Dr. Michael S. Lawson, *The Complete Handbook for Children's Ministry* (Nashville, TN: Thomas Nelson, Inc., 1993).
6. "A Safe Place for Children" seminar manual, 1998, International Network of Children's Ministry, Castle Rock, CO.
7. John Powell, Professor, Counseling Center, Michigan State University.
8. Church and the Law Update, June 1994.
9. Canadian Council of Christian Charities Bulletin #2, 1996, p. 6.

# RECRUITING MINISTRY VOLUNTEERS

The first step in recruiting volunteers is to establish a recruiting process. Such a process is not intended to restrict but rather to ensure safe and effective ministry to all age levels.

A pastoral staff member or appointed layperson should recruit volunteers. His or her responsibility should be to present names of prospective volunteers to the appointed or designated committee/board for approval prior to approaching the individual regarding a ministry assignment. All volunteers should be church members in good standing or adherents in harmony with the doctrines and principles of the church and should be regular attendees for at least six months. Once the committee/board has approved the volunteer and preliminary qualifications have been checked, the recruiter should then contact the prospective volunteer and oversee completion of the recruiting process.

## THE RECRUITING PROCESS

It is safe to say that the job of a recruiter is never done. Most church ministries and organizations dependent on volunteers are always in need of additional workers.

Properly screening potential volunteers is the first line of defense in providing a safe ministry environment. In order to be protected from liability, the church must show evidence that it has taken reasonable action in screening and supervising volunteers. If an abuse accusation occurs, the courts will look for a process by which the church screens volunteers before engaging them in service. A court can find the church negligent—and therefore legally liable—if it is less than systematic in its recruiting process. Therefore it is important that a recruitment process be established, approved and followed in every church. Accurate record keeping is crucial.

SAFE

PLACE

## A. Committee/Board Approval

All volunteers must first receive the approval of the designated committee/board. If the pastor or committee/board members know of reasons why a person would not be suitable for a volunteer position, final approval or denial of the appointment will be made only after further investigation. It is recommended that those who have been convicted of child abuse and subsequently restored be directed to ministries that do not involve direct contact with children or youth.

Once committee/board approval has been secured, the potential volunteer should be contacted and his or her interest in ministry assessed.

## B. Volunteer Personnel Form

The volunteer personnel form must be completed for all positions involving ministry to individuals at all age levels. The form requests personal, spiritual and health-related information. All forms should be kept in a permanent file and in such a manner that confidentiality will be maintained. This form is a critical screening step in the process of protecting both the church and those in its care from legal action if a case of abuse occurs in which a church volunteer is involved. (A recommended volunteer personnel form may be found in Appendix A.)

TRAINING TIPS

- Provide a copy of the volunteer personnel form for each class participant.
- Highlight key sections of the volunteer personnel form, emphasizing that all volunteers are being held to the same level of accountability.
- For personally sensitive issues, encourage volunteers to speak in confidence with the pastor or appointed person.
- Assure the students that confidentiality will be strictly maintained.

## C. Reference Check Record

Three personal references are requested on the volunteer personnel form. These references should exclude relatives and include at least one reference from outside the church. Teenaged volunteers should include the youth pastor (if applicable) as a reference. Each reference should be contacted by phone or in writing and asked to affirm the appointment of the volunteer. A record should be kept of the person making the phone call or written contact, the date of the call/contact and a summary of the reference's comments. (A recommended reference check record form may be found in Appendix B, a screening volunteers telephone script in Appendix C and a written reference response form in Appendix D.)

## D. Interview

An interview provides the appointed recruiter the opportunity to review important items from the volunteer personnel form with the prospective volunteer. This allows for follow-up questions and a better understanding of the applicant. The interview also allows the potential volunteer to ask questions about various ministries or about the church's protection policies. The information given in the interview will be available to the designated committee/board and, therefore, has limited confidentiality.

## E. Criminal History Check

The volunteer personnel form includes a statement that grants permission to pursue a criminal records check with local, state and government agencies. A records check may be made, if deemed necessary, for any volunteer. Such a check is strongly encouraged. Any records secured should be placed in the volunteer's placement file and considered confidential.

Background Verification Service: An excellent resource designed to offer verification assistance for local church leaders has been developed by Church Law & Tax Report and Secure Point (formerly known as the Pinkerton Service Group). For more information call 888.310.2558 and request the "Selecting and Screening Church Workers" brochure. For quicker, smoother service you may visit their Web site at <www.screennow.com>.

Legal counsel has advised the publisher that such a check is required for paid pastoral staff, day-care center workers and Christian school workers.

## F. Final Approval

Upon recommendation of the designated committee/board, the applicant should receive final approval for volunteer placement from the church governing board. Prior to final approval, the applicant should have completed the screening criteria: church membership or adherents in harmony with the doctrines and principles of the church, six-month attendance, volunteer personnel form, reference check, interview and crimi-nal records check (if necessary). (A recommended volunteer application approval process form may be found in Appendix E.)

Volunteers currently serving must be considered when implementing a new screening policy. While they should not be exempt from the new recruiting process, they should be allowed time to comply with these policies.

# three

# CREATING A SAFE ENVIRONMENT

A ll churches must be concerned for the safety of each and every person God has brought into their realm of ministry. At the same time, churches must be concerned with the safety and reputation of their volunteer leaders, teachers and workers. Once properly screened volunteers are working in church ministries, the next step in providing a safe and secure ministry environment is supervision of those volunteers. Carefully administered supervising procedures make it more difficult for abuse to occur. Supervising procedures also provide information to refute false accusations. Once again, the courts look for a systematic process by which the church supervises its volunteers.

## A. STAFFING AND SUPERVISING

### 1. Two-Adult Rule

A minimum of two adults should be present in any room except in the event of an emergency. This standard not only helps provide for a safe and loving classroom, it also gives volunteers more encouragement, creativity and flexibility. In addition, this arrangement allows for a gift-mix in each classroom that makes for a richer teaching environment. The arrangement may require that grade levels be combined. Smaller churches may need to use one adult with one teen helper.

### 2. Open Doors

Doors should have clear glass windows that allow for an easy view of the classroom activities without disrupting the teaching process.

If there is only one adult teacher in the classroom and the door does not have a glass window, it should be left slightly open.

### 3. Family Protection

It is recommended that immediate family members not work together in the same classroom. For those choosing to minister together, it is advised that, when possible, a third, unrelated volunteer be placed in the classroom.

SAFE

PLACE

15

4. Teacher/Student Ratios

   Adequate staffing is necessary to provide optimal care. The recommended ratios are:

   • One caregiver for every three infants (birth to twelve months)

   • One caregiver for every four toddlers or preschoolers

   • One caregiver for every eight to ten elementary-age children

Consideration should be given to training personal aides, as need may require, to assist individuals having disabling conditions.

5. Volunteer Age

   The use of adult volunteers (eighteen years of age and older) is recommended. However, some churches may find it necessary to use volunteers between the ages of twelve and eighteen. While teens should never care for children alone, it is beneficial to their spiritual development to allow teens to serve in appropriate team-teaching settings in ministry programs.

6. Supervision

   Supervisory staff should be in place to oversee the following:

   • Checking classrooms to ensure the room is properly staffed and functioning well

   • Monitoring hallways and exits to ensure that everyone is where they belong

   • Assisting visitors and newcomers in finding appropriate locations

   • Ensuring that suspicious individuals are properly approached and monitored

## TRAINING TIP

• Give a brief explanation for each of the six points listed above.

## B. Early Childhood/Elementary Considerations

1. Volunteer Identification

   All volunteers working with children should wear either a name tag or approved clothing (i.e., smock) that clearly identifies them as staff members to parents, visitors and newcomers.

2. Child Registration

Sign-in forms should be at the entrance of the nursery/classroom door. Parents should record their child's name, their names and their location during the service. Any special needs of the child should also be listed. The sign-in forms should be collected weekly and kept on file. In the case of an abuse allegation, these forms could be used to justify attendance. Security numbers and identification cards may also be used. Additionally, names and addresses of parents and children should be filed and carefully maintained. (A recommended child care sign-in form may be found in Appendix F.)

3. Volunteer Registration

Volunteer sign-in forms should be used in early childhood classrooms to record the name of each volunteer and the times he or she entered and exited the room. These forms should be gathered weekly and kept on file. In the case of an abuse allegation, the forms could be used to prove/disprove volunteer presence in the room. The forms also substantiate use of the two-adult rule. (A recommended volunteer sign-in form may be found in Appendix G.)

4. Releasing Children

The parent or guardian signing in a child is to be the one who picks up the child. A sign-out line for the parent to initial may be included on the sign-in form. Additionally, it is suggested that parents do not enter the nursery unless requested to do so. This better enables the child-care staff to maintain order and provide the level of security that parents would expect.

5. Diaper Changing

A diaper-changing procedure should be developed that utilizes standard precautions concerning blood-borne pathogens. The procedure should be posted near changing areas. (A recommended diaper-changing procedure may be found in Appendix H.)

The diaper-changing area should be located where at least one other worker can view the changing procedure.

It is highly recommended that only adult female volunteers be assigned to change diapers.

6. Rest Room Guidelines

We strongly recommend that parents take their children to visit the rest room prior to each class or service. This procedure should be communicated to parents at the beginning of each new school year and throughout the year.

a. Two adults should escort a group of children to the rest room. Some churches may not have two adults available for this duty. Therefore, we recommend that these churches appoint hallway or safety monitors (preferably female) to assist with rest room duties.

b. Classrooms should take scheduled rest room breaks.

c. Teen volunteers should not assist children in the rest room.

d. If just one child must go to the rest room, the adult volunteer should escort the child and prop the outside door open. The volunteer should then remain outside the door and wait for the child before escorting him or her back to the classroom. The volunteer should call the child's name if he or she is taking longer than seems necessary.

e. Volunteers and/or staff should never be alone with a child in an unsupervised rest room and never go into a cubicle with a child and shut the door.

f. If children need assistance, an adult may enter the rest room/cubicle only under the following guidelines:

   i. A second adult must be within visual contact. If this is not possible, another adult should at least be informed of the situation and notified when a volunteer is leaving with a child and when returning.

   ii. Only women should assist girls or boys in the rest room. In light of the fact that most abusers are male, and for the protection of male volunteers from false accusation, it would be wise for men to avoid assisting children in using the rest room.

   iii. The outside rest room door must be propped open. The adult must stand in the open cubicle doorway.

7. Clean Hands

Proper hand washing is one of the basics to good health and is one of the key standard precautions in the prevention of the spread of disease. Children and adults should be taught and reminded of the proper hand-washing procedure. Good old soap and warm water is adequate as long as twenty seconds is taken to wash all hand surfaces, including in between fingers. Drying hands with disposable towels is best. Use the towel to turn off the faucet, then discard the towel in the appropriate receptacle.

Teaching children to sing the ABC song while washing will help them to wash long enough. Teachers, caregivers and students should be trained to wash before eating or handling bottles, after rest room use and as the diaper-changing and standard precautions procedures suggest.

While the use of antibacterial soap is popular, it isn't necessary. In fact, many children are sensitive to antibacterial ingredients. If a sink is not available nearby, it is advisable to make non-soap hand disinfectants available for students and caregivers to use.

It would be a good idea to make copies of the poster on hand washing in Appendix I and post them in rest rooms and nurseries.

- Give a brief explanation for each of the seven points listed above.

TRAINING TIP

## C. HEALTH AND SAFETY GUIDELINES

1. Well Child Policy

   A child who is ill and could therefore expose other children and workers to illness should not be received into the nursery or classroom. Some signs of illness are unusual fatigue or irritability, coughing, sneezing, runny nose and eyes, fever, vomiting, diarrhea or inflamed mouth and throat. (PLEASE NOTE: Coughing, sneezing, runny nose and eyes can also be symptoms of allergies. Be sure to check with parents as to the cause of the symptoms before denying the child entry into the nursery.) A health criteria policy should be posted. A sample may be found in Appendix J.

2. Medications

   a. Volunteers are not to give or apply any medications. If a child needs medication, the parent must give it.

   b. No medication should be left in the classroom, with a volunteer worker or with the child.

   c. In extreme cases (allergies, asthma), arrangements for the administration of medication should be made with written instructions and permission from the parent. Medication should be in its original prescription bottle/package, which should have administration instructions and the child's name clearly indicated. Volunteers should be sure to notify parents when they pick up their child that medication has been administered.

   d.  Medication also includes the application of baby powder and ointments during diaper changing. These topical medications should not be used unless a doctor's written order is provided and parents instruct volunteers to do so on the sign-in form. Only use topical medications supplied by the parent.

3.  Emergencies

   a.  Procedures for emergency situations (fire, tornado, etc.) should be reviewed regularly during volunteer training seminars. These procedures as well as a planned route of escape to safety are to be posted in a visible place in each classroom.

   b.  An infectious disease kit must be kept in each of the organization's classrooms and vehicles for handling cuts, bloody noses, vomiting, etc. All volunteers should be trained in the proper use of the kit's contents. Each kit should contain a pair of disposable vinyl gloves, a foil packet with a disinfectant towelette, two or three 4" x 4" gauze pads for blood absorption and one or two adhesive bandages. Place contents in a zip-closure plastic bag.

   c.  In addition to the infectious disease kits, a first aid box should be available on each floor level of the church building and in any church-owned vehicle. Each first aid kit should contain a microshield CPR mask, instant ice packs and quantities of the items mentioned above in the infectious disease kits.

   d.  When an injury, accident or medical emergency occurs, the parent(s) of the child involved should be contacted immediately.

   e.  Any accident resulting in injury should be reported to the ministry leader in charge. A completed accident report should be submitted to the designated leader in a timely manner. See Appendix K for an accident and injury report form.

TRAINING TIPS

• Give a brief explanation for each of the three points listed above.
• Assemble an infectious disease kit to show as an example. Identify and explain the items included in the kit.

4. Procedures for Dealing with Blood and Body Fluids

   a. The Occupational Safety and Health Administration's (OSHA) Final Rule for Occupational Exposure to Blood-Borne Pathogens (29 CFR 1910.1030) became effective nationwide on March 6, 1992. OSHA authority includes private sector employers who employ one or more employees, so this includes churches. Substantial fines can be levied against employers who do not comply with OSHA standards. Although this OSHA mandate applies to employers and employees specifically, we feel it is important to include these procedures in all areas of the church. Instituting a blood-borne pathogen policy will mean extra paperwork and record keeping, training of volunteers and purchasing of appropriate supplies. However, the benefits of this policy will outweigh any difficulties, and will ensure a much safer ministry environment for students and volunteers.

      Please review the document entitled "Responding to OSHA's Final Rule for 'Occupational Exposure to Blood-Borne Pathogens,' " (see Appendix L). Also review the "Excerpt from: 'Clarification of the Standard on Occupational Exposure to Blood-Borne Pathogens, 29 CFR 1910.1030' " (see Appendix M). These appendices will provide necessary information to assist your understanding of blood-borne pathogen issues, will guide your church's formation of policies and will give information needed to train volunteers.

   b. Definition of Terms

      i. A *blood-borne pathogen* is any microorganism or virus found in blood and other body fluids (urine, feces, vomit, semen, vaginal secretions) that can cause disease. The primary concerns with blood-borne pathogens are with HIV (which causes AIDS), HBV (which causes hepatitis B) and HCV (which causes hepatitis C).

     ii. *Standard precautions* are hygienic measures used to inhibit the spread of blood-borne pathogens. All blood and body fluids should be treated as a source of contamination and infection.

    iii. *Occupational exposure* is defined as the likelihood of skin, eye, mucous membrane or parenteral (skin-penetrated) contact with blood or body fluids.

   c. Develop a Written Plan

      An exposure control plan should include:

      • identification of employees (volunteers) with high-risk tasks;

- records of hepatitis B vaccinations;
- procedures for implementing standard precautions;
- exposure incident reporting and follow-up; and
- training.

d.  Identify Occupational Exposure

Most church employees and volunteers will have a possible risk of exposure. These people include teachers, child-care workers and custodians. The church is required to provide training and post-exposure hepatitis B vaccinations for employees in the event an exposure occurs. Similar considerations may be provided for volunteers as well.

e.  Train Volunteers

All volunteers should receive training in the basic knowledge of blood-borne pathogens and in the logic behind church policy concerning such issues. This is a crucial step in helping them to understand why they should follow new procedures. The new procedures (i.e., diaper-changing procedures) should be explained and demonstrated. Appendices L and M will provide ample information for the formulation of training materials on blood-borne pathogens.

f.  Infectious Disease Kits

Infectious disease kits provide volunteers with the equipment to respond confidently, quickly and safely to accidents involving body fluids. These kits are a simple solution to providing standard precautions. A kit should be placed in each classroom, activity area and church-owned vehicle.

**TRAINING TIP**

- While this is a very detailed section that key staff members will want to understand, it is recommended as an advanced or continuing education option for other leaders, teachers and workers.

## D. Responding to an Injury or Illness

1.  Separate the injured or ill student from other children.

2. Isolate the area where any blood or body fluid may have dropped on carpet, toys, chairs, etc.

3. Keep other students from having contact with the body fluid.

4. Locate the infectious disease kit and put on vinyl gloves.

5. Attend to the student as needed using contents of the infectious disease kit.

6. Clean the room following standard precaution guidelines. This is best accomplished by a custodian.

7. Place all soiled gauze, bandages and wrappers into the zip-closure bag. Remove vinyl gloves and place into the bag. Seal and dispose of the bag in a plastic-lined trash container.

8. Wash hands carefully with soap and warm water.

- Roleplay a common situation such as a nose bleed, vomiting, etc., allowing class participants to demonstrate the proper response.

TRAINING TIP

## E. HOUSEKEEPING

1. Nursery/Classrooms

All changing table surfaces, toys, cribs, table tops, etc., must be cleaned with a disinfecting solution at the conclusion of each session. Develop and post a diaper-changing procedure (see Appendix H for an example).

2. Custodial Cleaning

Proper cleaning practices using appropriate-strength cleaning agents are required. A variety of job-appropriate cleaners can be found by contacting a janitorial supply company.

## F. ARCHITECTURAL CONSIDERATIONS

We recommend that churches review the following suggestions when building or remodeling nurseries and children's classrooms.

1. Windows and Doors

   a. Interior windows allow for easy viewing of classroom activities by parents and super-visors.

   b. Doors should have windows. Consider installing two-way glass in them. The view through these windows should never be obstructed.

   c. Dutch doors are preferred in rooms used for the care of babies and toddlers. Use of these doors can facilitate the open-door policy without compromising the safety of the children.

2. Rest Rooms

   a. Rest room facilities located in preschool rooms remove the need for children to leave the classroom.

   b. Windows on preschool rest room doors enable helpers to assist the child while in view of other adults.

   c. Child-size toilets and sinks make it possible for children to use the rest room with little assistance.

3. Nursery/Preschool Rooms

   a. Nursery rooms should be conveniently located near the sanctuary and on ground level with easy access to an outside exit.

   b. Room sizes of 1,100 square feet are ideal.

   c. Diaper-changing tables should be in full view.

   d. Doors should be secured from the inside to prevent anyone from entering unnoticed.

   e. Nursery sleeping rooms should have a door with a window and should be monitored with a radio transmitter.

   f. All electrical outlets should be covered with outlet plug covers or tamper-resistant wall plates.

   g. For their safety, children should be grouped by developmental stages.

## G. Proper Display of Affection

Physical touch is an important element in the communication of love and care. It is an essential part of the nurturing process that should be characteristic of ministry with students. Volunteers need to be aware of, and sensitive to, the special and differing needs and preferences of each individual. Physical contact should be age- and developmentally appropriate and is most appropriate when done publicly.

1. Appropriate Touch

    The following guidelines are recommended as pure, genuine and positive displays of God's love:

    a. Meet children at their eye level by bending down or sitting.

    b. Listen to individuals with your ears, eyes and heart.

    c. Hold the child's hand while listening or speaking to him or when walking to an activity.

    d. Putting an arm around the shoulder of an individual when comforting, quieting or greeting is an appropriate way to hug. This side-to-side type of hug should only be done in public.

    e. A light touch to a hand, shoulder or back when encouraging is acceptable.

    f. Gently hold the shoulders or chin of a child when redirecting the child's behavior. This helps the child focus on what you are saying and is helpful with children who have Attention Deficit Hyperactive Disorder.

    g. Hold a preschool child who is crying.

2. Inappropriate Touch

    The following types of touch must be avoided:

    a. Kissing a child or coaxing a child to kiss you.

    b. Extended hugging and tickling, or prolonged physical contact of any kind.

    c. Touching a child in any area that would be covered by a bathing suit (exception: properly assisting a child in the rest room).

    d. Carrying an older child or sitting him or her on your lap.

    e. Being alone with a child.

    f. Giving a full contact, body-to-body hug.

- Since this is such an important area, make a fill-in-the-blank worksheet using the points listed above so learners will have a take-home copy for reference.
- Demonstrate appropriate touch.

TRAINING TIPS

# H. Special Events and Overnight Policies

Teachers are encouraged to have special class activities in their homes, to plan social activities and to involve their pupils in field trips and service projects. However, precautions need to be taken with these activities. The safety guidelines outlined below should be followed.

1. Field Trips, Special Events and Personal Appointments
   a. Off-site activities should be preapproved by church leaders who must fill out a church activity report form (see Appendix N). Parents should be notified at least one week prior to the outing.
   b. Parental consent and medical release forms are required for each child participating. (A recommended parental consent statement may be found in Appendix O. A recommended medical release form may be found in Appendix P.) Forms must be kept in leaders' possession during trips and events.
   c. Parents should be well informed of the activities scheduled for each event.
   d. All trips and outings should be supervised by a minimum of two approved, unrelated adult leaders.
   e. All one-on-one appointments should be preapproved by both a parent and a ministry supervisor.

2. Transportation
   a. All drivers transporting children during an activity must have valid driver's licenses and current automobile insurance.
   b. The number of occupants in the vehicle should not exceed the number of seat belts. Seat belts must be worn.
   c. Church leaders must contact their insurance company regarding the minimum and maximum age ranges and other requirements, to ensure that coverage is in effect for all approved drivers. This must be done for all vehicles and all drivers—privately owned, church owned and rental vehicles.
   d. As often as possible have parents transport their own children to and from ministry activities.

3. Overnight Events
   a. All overnight events must be preapproved by church leaders (see church activity report in Appendix N).

b. Parental consent and medical release forms are required for each child participating (see Appendices O and P). Forms must be kept in leaders' possession during all events.

c. Parents should be well informed of the activities scheduled for each event.

d. All supervising adults must be approved volunteers.

e. There should be two adult leaders for every ten children. Every leader should have an assigned group of children for which he is responsible. An appropriate male/female, leader/student ratio is required.

f. Consult your church insurance policy or agent to ensure that liability coverage includes any off-site activities. Occasionally some activities require additional insurance coverage or riders.

## TRAINING TIP

• Distribute and review copies of Appendices N, O and P.

## I. DISCIPLINE POLICY

A classroom discipline policy should be developed so that volunteers are able to deal with behavior difficulties in a caring and consistent manner. *A hands-off approach is a must.* Volunteers should be trained in using the discipline policy so they understand the importance of its proper use and are prepared to use it. Proper discipline includes both preventative care and corrective action, and it also helps create a healthy learning environment.

1. *Reward* good behavior. Immediate praise and recognition for positive actions are effective ways to encourage more of the same. Inform parents when a child does well or shows improvement.

2. *Remind* the student of proper classroom behavior. Remind him/her of the classroom rules and what is expected.

3. *Redirect* the student. Move him/her to a different situation or area. Separate the child from others when he/she is having difficulty behaving.

4. *Remove* the student from the group using a time-out chair within the classroom and in view of both volunteers. After an appropriate explanation of what is wrong with the child's behavior is given, give him/her several minutes to sit alone (the child's age should equal the time-out minutes). When the child is settled, invite him/her to rejoin the group.

5. *Return* the student to a parent. If steps 1 through 4 fail to change behavior, the child should be taken to a parent for the remainder of the class. After class, the teacher will explain the problem to the parents and reassure the child that he/she is welcome to join the class next time. The teacher will report the action to the appropriate supervisor.

6. Suggested Classroom Manners

   (Make a copy of the poster provided in Appendix Q and post in all rooms.)

   a. Be kind to one another.

   b. Pay attention and listen.

   c. Follow instructions.

   d. Talk one at a time.

   e. Keep hands and feet to yourself.

## Training Tips

- Briefly review the five "R's."
- Hand out copies of the classroom manners poster and encourage their promotion and display in every class setting.

## J. Internet Access and Web Sites

The explosive expansion of the Internet and World Wide Web has led to the proliferation of pornographic, illegal and dangerous material and has made it readily available to anyone with a computer. Because there are no legal restrictions on content whatsoever, it is incumbent upon every church to protect any computers or networks that are hooked up to the Internet. Fortunately, various filtered Web-access technologies have the potential to make the Web cleaner than broadcast television.

1. Internet Access

    a. *Client-based filtering*. This was the first approach to filtering and can still work well in a supervised environment such as a managed church server. The filtering software is loaded onto your local computer and must be updated regularly by subscription to a service. This can be done automatically over the Web.

    **Disadvantages:**

- It must be updated regularly to work properly, since new Web sites go on-line by the thousands every day.
- It is easily defeated at the local computer by disabling the software, unless administrated on a network from a secure server.
- One-time purchase cost for software.
- Monthly update subscription cost.

    **Examples:**

- NetNanny at www.netnanny.com.
- CyberPatrol at www.surfcontrol.com (800.828.2608).

    b. *Proxy-based filtering*. This method routes your web access through a remote filter service which is updated automatically. It allows you to use an inexpensive local Internet service provider (ISP) and still get reliable filtering. Blocks chatrooms and newsgroups and may filter Web searches.

    **Disadvantages:**

- May add cost.
- Is easily defeated at the local computer by disabling the proxy.

    **Examples:**

- Family Click, Realtime Sentry, We-Blocker, BSafe Online can all be found at www.crosswalk.com under the "Internet Safety" link.
- Covenant Promotions at www.pornblocker.com (888.564.7555).
- American Family Online at www.afo.net.

    c. *Server-based filtering*. This is the most secure and reliable method, since filtering is done at the ISP and non-filtered access is blocked. It blocks access to chatrooms and newsgroups unless provided by the filtered ISP. May filter searches. Some providers (like America Online) have on-line services as well. Your local unfiltered ISP may be willing to add a filter to your service for an additional charge (see the Bess Internet Retriever at www.n2h2.com).

**Disadvantages:**

- There may not be a toll-free local access number in your area.
- May cost more than unfiltered access.
- Subscriber can obtain a temporary authorized access password and defeat the system.

**Examples:**

- American Family Online at www.afo.net.
- Covenant Promotions at www.pornblocker.com (888.564.7555).
- Integrity Online at www.integrityonline.com (866.449.1706).
- CleanWeb at www.cleanweb.net.

d. *Filtering by on-line services.* America Online provides "Parental Controls" both for its site and the Web. This method is similar in outcome to proxy-based filtering. Check with other providers such as Prodigy, CompuServe, etc., for filtering information.

**Disadvantages:**

- The parental controls work well, but full access is available to the main password holder or anyone who obtains the password.
- Will not work with other proxy service providers.

2. Informational Web Sites

- **www.childsexualabuse.org**: An excellent Web site for articles, policies and trends in dealing with child sexual abuse. Includes links to other child safety sites.
- **www.iclonline.com**: A good source for training materials on reducing the risk of child sexual abuse in your church. Also available from Christian Ministry Resources, P.O. Box 1098, Matthews, NC 28106 or by calling 800.222.1840.
- **www.calib.com/nccanch**: National Clearinghouse on Child Abuse and Neglect Information. A national resource for professionals and others seeking information on child abuse and neglect and child welfare.

3. Web Site Development

When developing a Web site for your local church or organization it is important that a signed release form be obtained from anyone whose picture may be used in this public way. A parent or guardian must sign for minors (see Appendix R for sample release form).

# four

# RESPONDING TO ALLEGATIONS OF ABUSE

## A. BE PREPARED IN ADVANCE

Realistically, no practical prevention strategy is 100 percent effective. An accusation of abuse could occur in any church. Because of this possibility, every church needs to develop a plan or strategy to respond to such an allegation. The church should not try to navigate a crisis situation without a compass to guide it. Wrong actions in response to an allegation of abuse could magnify the pain and liability inherent in such a case. An effective response strategy recognizes the following underlying principles:

1. All allegations need to be taken seriously.
2. Situations must be handled forthrightly, with due respect for an individual's privacy and confidentiality.
3. Full cooperation must be given to civil authorities under the guidance of the church's lawyer.
4. Appropriate care must be shown for the well-being of alleged victims.
5. The alleged victim should not be held responsible in any way.
6. The church's insurance agent should be contacted immediately.

## B. CREATE A RESPONSE PLAN

In light of the above principles, a thorough response plan should be developed. If possible, it should be reviewed with the church's lawyer and insurance agent.

1. Maintain Adequate Records

Always have adequate records of volunteer workers' applications, references and screening forms. They should be up-to-date and accessible. Records should be kept at least five years after the conclusion of a person's volunteer ministry.

2. Select a Spokesperson

   Designate a specific spokesperson for the church. If allegations of abuse occur, this person should be able to speak to the media and the congregation in a discreet, informed, truthful and diplomatic way. Everyone involved in the ministry of the church should know who this person is and should not attempt to respond to allegations themselves. All inquiries should be referred to the appointed spokesperson. The media will most likely want to interview church leaders, but these individuals might not have experience in responding to such inquiries. Conflicting and contradictory statements can be reported, and the public could develop a negative impression of the church. These potential problems can be avoided if only one person is designated to speak for the church.

3. Know Your Reporting Obligations

   Know your state's reporting requirements. States differ in terms of behaviors that should be reported and who is obligated to report suspected abuse. This information is available from the Department of Health and Human Services, a lawyer's office or local law enforcement agencies. In addition, the church will need to determine which local agencies are responsible for investigating possible abuse.

4. Use a Reporting Procedure

   Develop a clear reporting procedure for all programs that work with students (see chapter 5 for the section on reporting procedures). Workers should be instructed as to what behaviors should be reported and to whom they should report. Workers should be assured that state law protects them from liability when they report actual or suspected abuse, so long as they do not act maliciously.

5. Prepare a Position Statement

   Develop a clear position statement regarding child abuse, including the policies and established safeguards. This statement can be released if an allegation of abuse occurs. Having a carefully prepared statement is better than making no comment. This is an opportunity to influence public opinion positively by emphasizing an awareness of the problem of child abuse, a concern for victims and the extensive steps the church has taken to reduce the risk and provide a safe place for students. Let the media know that the church takes the risk of child abuse seriously and that the church has acted responsibly. Describe all the precautions the church has taken and the policies the church has implemented. *This is no time for silence or "no comment."* Do not surrender the pulpit to those who will criticize and condemn the church. Here is an example of such a statement:

> It is always tragic when children are abused or exploited. _____ Church is aware of the ever-growing nature of child abuse and the harm that is done to the victims. We have taken every precaution to protect the students entrusted to our care. Our paid staff and volunteers are carefully screened before beginning ministry in our church. Training occurs to inform our ministry staff about the various policies implemented to provide for the safety of our students. We have also reviewed with our staff what to watch for and how to report any suspicious behavior relating to the abuse of students. We are distressed by any accusation of child abuse. We will do everything in our power to address this situation. For the welfare of those involved, all information has been directed to the Department of Health and Human Services.

*Be prepared* to explain the specific precautions, the screening process and the training that the church utilizes to provide a safe and secure environment.

6. **Don't Engage in Denial, Minimization or Blame**

   Many churches, when confronted with an allegation of abuse, respond in one or more of the following ways:

   a. Deny that the incident occurred despite clear evidence to the contrary.

   b. Acknowledge that the incident occurred, but minimize it. For example, a church leader may say, "It only happened once," or "It wasn't that serious."

   c. Blame the victim or the victim's family.

   *These responses are all inappropriate and should be avoided.*

7. **Use a Lawyer**

   Always have the church's lawyer present while answering any investigative questions from the police or social service agencies. The accused should follow the same procedure with his or her lawyer.

8. **Don't Be Accusatory**

   Avoid spelling out the details of an accusation in a public interview.

9. **Work with Denomination and Insurance Company**

   Contact the denominational office and obtain information about the specific guidelines and procedures it endorses. Work closely with an insurance company.

## C. When an Allegation Occurs

In the case of an actual allegation, follow these guidelines:

1. Immediately record the facts of the incident (i.e., persons present, phone calls, correspondence, etc.).

2. Document all of the church's efforts at handling the incident.

3. Report the incident immediately to the church's lawyer, insurance agent and denominational officials. Don't try to handle this without professional outside assistance. The accused should do the same.

4. Following the guidance of the church's lawyer, contact the proper civil authorities. Don't attempt an in-depth investigation. This should be left to professionals who are familiar with these cases.

5. Take the allegations seriously and reach out to the victim and the victim's family. Showing care and support helps to prevent further hurt. Extend whatever pastoral resources are needed, and remember that the care and safety of the victim is the first priority. Don't prejudge the situation. In some instances, churches have responded in a negative or nonsupportive manner to the alleged victim. This type of response can increase the anger and pain of the victim and the victim's family. Future reconciliation will be more difficult and the possibility of damaging litigation increases.

6. Treat the accused with dignity and support. If the accused is a church worker, that person should be relieved temporarily of his or her duties until the investigation is finished (see Galatians 6:1-2).

7. Use the text of the prepared public statement to answer the press and to convey news to the congregation. Be careful to safeguard the privacy and confidentiality of all involved.

**Training Tips**

- Present the "Plan to Respond," which is based on the above information and input from your insurance carrier and legal council, so everyone will know his personal responsibility.
- Emphasize that no one should make a promise that cannot be kept. (He should not promise that he will not tell anyone, because there may be a point at which he is required to speak with the appropriate authorities about the incident.)

## D. Key Contacts

Lawyer to be contacted: _____

Phone number:   (      ) _____


Insurance agent to be contacted: _____

Phone number:   (      ) _____


Designated spokesperson for the church: _____

Phone number:   (      ) _____


This chapter was adapted with permission from *Reducing the Risk of Child Sexual Abuse in Your Church*, copyright 1993 by Church Law and Tax Report, Matthews, NC.

# REPORTING PROCEDURES

## A. OBLIGATION TO REPORT

If church workers have any concerns regarding the safety of a student, they should report to their ministry head and the pastoral staff. The pastoral staff should then follow through in contacting the Department of Health and Human Services. At this point in time, it may be advisable for the pastoral staff to contact a lawyer. Subsequent to these steps of reporting, the church's denominational office should be informed of the situation.

1. Who Must Report

Every state has mandatory reporting laws that govern the reporting of child abuse. Church workers need to be aware of these laws and other specific guidelines relating to the reporting process. Although a church worker may not be in the position of *having* to report the abuse, everyone who has reasonable grounds to believe a student has been or is being abused needs to report the possible abuse. The report should be made to his or her ministry head and the pastoral staff, who will then report to the Department of Health and Human Services or your local Child Protective Services agency. For working definitions of abuse and neglect, see the Understanding Child Abuse section (page 7) of this book.

Social workers designated to receive reports are trained to investigate and assess the need for intervention. Other professionals must not assume this function. No action will be taken against a person making a report unless it is made maliciously or without reasonable grounds for belief.

2. What to Report

Any items of obvious concern relating to child abuse or neglect should immediately be reported to the ministry head and the pastoral staff. All volunteers and paid staff who are involved in ministry to students should report any such items of which they have knowledge or have observed within the scope of their duties. It is not the responsibility of the reporting person or the paid staff to substantiate any allegations or suspicions. The following list entitled "Recognizing Signs of Abuse" will provide tips on what to watch for (see Appendix S for copy):

**Recognizing Signs of Abuse**

a. Unexplained bruises, burns, fractures or abrasions (often in various stages of healing)

b. Consistent lack of supervision

c. Consistent hunger, inappropriate dress, poor hygiene or unattended medical needs

d. Extremes of aggression or withdrawal

e. Moves with discomfort and shies away from physical contact

f. Wearing clothing inappropriate for the weather in order to cover body

g. Withdrawn, depressed, listless

h. Torn, stained or bloody underwear

i. Irritation of the mouth, genital or anal area

j. Difficulty sitting or walking

k. Inappropriate sex play, acting out seductiveness or promiscuity

l. Sudden changes in school performance, appetite or perceived self-worth

Abuse or neglect need not have occurred for a student to be in need of protection. It is not necessary to wait until a student has been harmed to intervene. When abuse or neglect can be reasonably anticipated and there are reasonable grounds to believe a student is in need of protection, the necessity of reporting applies. If a volunteer or employee has questions about a specific incident, an anonymous phone call can be placed to the Department of Health and Human Services or your local Child Protective Services (CPS) agency to clarify whether or not the given situation constitutes a reportable offense.[1] To maintain anonymity be sure to use a public phone or a private phone that blocks outgoing phone numbers.

3. Confidentiality

In these matters it is important to keep the information confidential at all times. Therefore, all suspicions of abuse should be confided only to the ministry head and pastoral staff. It is the responsibility of the pastoral staff to contact the local office of the Department of Health and Human Services.

Although physicians, clergy and lawyers consider their professional relationships confidential as part of the solicitor-client privilege, they are not exempt from the duty to report child abuse or neglect.

4. Responding to the Student

When a student first comes to you, be sure to take his or her word seriously. Don't deny the problem, but stay calm and listen to the student. Give emotional support, reminding the student that he or she is not at fault and that he or she was right in telling you about the problem. *Do not* promise the student you will not tell anyone.

5. Report Form

Use a suspected abuse report form as found in Appendix T. These forms may be obtained from the ministry head or pastoral staff. Fill out the report form and submit it to a member of the pastoral staff.

6. Summary of Steps

a. Gently affirm the student.

b. Immediately report any suspected abuse to the appropriate ministry head and the pastoral staff. Complete the suspected abuse report form.

c. It is the responsibility of the pastoral staff to report to the local office of the Department of Health and Human Services by telephone, letter or in person. Since time requirements may differ from state to state, it is imperative to contact the Department of Health and Human Services in your state to determine your responsibility. Absolute confidentiality is maintained by the Department of Health and Human Services.

- Distribute and review the suspected abuse report form as found in Appendix T.
- For review, use the provided worksheet in the Training Ministry Volunteers section and/or the "Recognizing Signs of Abuse" chart as found in Appendix S.

TRAINING TIPS

## B. PROTECTION FROM LIABILITY

Church personnel are required to immediately report to the Department of Health and Human Services any suspected case of child abuse. It is not a breach of confidence between church personnel and the student involved. No person is personally liable for anything done or omitted in good faith in the exercise of this responsibility. Church leaders are accountable to God to protect all individuals—children, youth and adult. Although the church desires to protect the parents as much as legally possible from undue interference by outside authorities into their families, the protection of students from abuse is even more important. The church should follow the principles of submitting to governing authorities (Romans 13:1), while at the same time it should help parents to exercise discipline that is consistent with the Scriptures and is in the best interest of their children.

## C. Report Follow-Up

A confidential written report with conclusions and action taken should always be made by the pastor who received the suspected abuse report form. Both the suspected abuse report form (Appendix T) and the suspected abuse follow-up report form (Appendix U) should be kept in a confidential personnel file.

## D. Church Discipline

A church or Christian organization should practice discipline according to Matthew 18:15-17 and in keeping with any denominational or organizational policy on discipline. The senior pastor or CEO should be knowledgeable regarding the denominational or organizational policy on discipline.

## Conclusion

The church must avoid any undue interference when a report of child abuse has been filed with the Department of Health and Human Services. The church should ask the Department of Health and Human Services how it can assist in helping and supporting the hurting student and his or her family. The church should maintain frequent communication and supportive relationships with those suspected or guilty of abuse as long as these persons exhibit a willingness to listen, change and look to Christ for help. This does not exclude the need for hurting individuals, the victims, the accused and their families to receive professional counseling.

### Endnote

1. You can call Childhelp's National Child Abuse Hotline at 1-800-4-A-CHILD (800-422-4453) TDD: 1-800-2-A-CHILD to get the reporting number for your state. Childhelp USA is a nonprofit agency which can provide reporting numbers, and has hotline counselors who can provide referrals.

# six

# ADDRESSING THE ISSUES OF COMMUNICABLE DISEASES

## POLICY STATEMENTS

The world in which we live requires church leaders to seriously consider the issues of communicable diseases and their influence on local church ministry. The following are several policy statements prepared by various churches to challenge your thinking in this area. They are intended to provoke thinking and to provide a starting point for discussion. *They are not intended to be copied verbatim.* These statements represent churches of different sizes and various geographical locations. Permission has been granted to use these statements in this manual.

Prayerfully review and consider these examples, then be encouraged to establish a proper communicable disease policy for your church.

The policy statements appear in the following order:

1. A Statement from the Elders on HIV (the AIDS Virus) and Our Church's Response to Those Infected (First Evangelical Free Church)
2. Infection Control Policy and Procedures—Preschool Ministry (Christ Community Church)
3. Infection Control Procedures (Christ Community Church)
4. AIDS/Communicable Disease Policy (Lombard Bible Church)
5. A Statement from the Elders on HIV (the AIDS Virus) and Our Church's Response to Those Infected (Grace Church)
6. Policy on AIDS (Westmont Alliance Church)
7. Policy on AIDS—Section A—Guidelines (Westgate Chapel)
8. Policy on AIDS—Section B—Procedures for Handling Blood and Body Spills (Westgate Chapel)

# A Statement from the Elders on HIV (the AIDS Virus) and Our Church's Response to Those Infected
### *First Evangelical Free Church*

It is the responsibility of First Evangelical Free Church (FEFC) to encourage righteousness in the way that we corporately and individually demonstrate the breadth and length and height and depth of Christ's love to all of God's creation (Ephesians 3:14-19). Because of the presence of growing numbers of persons with AIDS in our society and the fears that many have about having casual contact with such persons, the Board of Elders of First Evangelical Free Church has adopted the following policy on AIDS to apply to the life of the church.

Regardless of the factors that may have led to the contracting of a particular disease, Christians are called to have compassion on all persons in need. Because we are followers of Jesus Christ, we must follow His example and teaching, as well as those of the Old and New Testament writers, in showing comfort and compassion to those who suffer from HIV disease. Just as Jesus showed compassion on those with leprosy (the HIV disease of His day), so must we show concern, compassion and Christ's love, and attempt to comfort those who may have this equally dreaded disease of our day and society. Colossians 3:12 urges us as God's chosen ones to be full of compassion, kindness and gentleness to those afflicted ones about us.

Acquired Immune Deficiency Syndrome (AIDS) is a serious, life-threatening condition that is not transmissible by casual contact. The best scientific evidence indicates that AIDS is caused by a virus known as HIV (human immunodeficiency virus), which is transmitted through the exchange of blood or semen by infected sexual partners, contaminated needles, contaminated blood or by infected mothers to their infants.

Medical knowledge about AIDS is developing, and thus is incomplete. It is almost certainly true that infection with the HIV virus takes a multiplicity of forms, some disabling and some not, varying not only from individual to individual, but also from one phase to another within the same individual. From what is known today, AIDS reduces the body's immune response, leaving the infected person vulnerable to life-threatening infections and malignancies.

In responding to the knowledge that someone attending FEFC has been infected with the AIDS virus, the Board of Elders will be guided by current medical knowledge, the known behavior of Jesus Christ and the principles of compassion and ministry established in the Bible.

An individual who has been diagnosed as being HIV-positive or who has AIDS would be treated with the same compassion as any other individual attending FEFC. In general, FEFC will not reject or ostracize anyone who is HIV-positive or who has AIDS, as long as that individual presents no real threat to the safety of others in the congregation. The confidentiality of HIV-positive individuals will be determined case by case based on the risk of potential exposure to others within the church.

In the case of infants or small children who are HIV-positive, U.S. Public Health Service guidelines are being followed. Nursery and children's workers will be trained accordingly.

We acknowledge that there are innocent victims who contract AIDS and other diseases through no fault of their own, such as health care workers, those who contract HIV through blood transfusions, rape and babies born to HIV-positive mothers. Due to the fact that AIDS has been spread in our nation and world primarily through behavior that is immoral and/or illegal (sexual immorality and drug abuse), we must affirm the biblical teaching that sexual intimacy is to be experienced only in the committed relationship of heterosexual marriage. Other kinds of sexual behavior are not only dishonoring to God but bear specific consequences of spiritual guilt and physical disease. The only "safe sex" is sex that is according to the plan of God. The abuse of drugs invites a variety of tragic consequences.

# Infection Control Policy and Procedures—
# Preschool Ministry
### *Christ Community Church*

## A. Introduction

It is the church's intent, as far as possible and within the scope of current knowledge, to protect all concerned parties from accidental exposure to the viruses that cause hepatitis B, Acquired Immune Deficiency Syndrome (AIDS) and other blood-borne communicable diseases.

By the very nature of preschool activity, diapered infants and toddlers and normal infant mouthing behavior, preschoolers are naturally exposed to a higher rate of infection than are other children. Infections such as diarrhea and hepatitis A are primarily spread by a fecal/oral route, meaning there is a higher spread among children who are in diapers. Infections such as serious forms of meningitis, influenza and most respiratory infections are spread by contact with respiratory secretions. Infections such as pink eye, impetigo, scabies, lice, ringworm and chicken pox are spread by person-to-person contact. Fever blisters (herpes) are spread by contact with saliva. Cytomegalovirus, a viral infection often without symptoms in children, but one which can cause birth defects in unborn babies, is spread through urine and saliva. So far as is now known by medical science, hepatitis B and AIDS are spread by contact with blood (transfusions, across the placenta in the unborn baby and through the birth process) and intimate contact (sexual intercourse and possibly breast feeding). There have been no known causes of hepatitis B or AIDS spread in day-care centers and no documented spread through daily living activities within families.

In order to minimize the spread of any infectious disease within the preschool area and to ensure the health and safety of all children and caregivers, the following procedures will be followed.

## B. Specific Procedures

1. Disposable gloves shall be worn by a caregiver when changing diapers, in accompanying a child to the toilet and in potential contact with blood (a cut or a bloody nose). Disposable gloves will be changed between each new child contact. In the event that

an emergency precludes the use of gloves when in contact with blood, the caregiver shall thoroughly clean the skin with soap and water.

2. Diapers shall be changed in the child's own crib or on a nonporous surface that is sanitized after each use.

3. Strict hand washing is of the utmost importance in the prevention of the spread of infection. Therefore, caregivers are required to wash hands after each diaper change, after accompanying a child to the toilet, after assisting a child to wipe his/her nose, after contact with blood, after toileting, after contact with his/her own nasal secretions and before food preparation. Caregivers should make sure that a child's hands are washed after toileting, after use of tissues for wiping eyes and nose and before eating. Disposable towels will be used after hand washing.

4. When an infant or toddler is seen to put an object into his/her mouth, this object shall be cleaned with a disinfecting solution before being returned to the "clean toy" container.

5. A disinfecting solution made of one part household bleach to 10 parts water (made daily) shall be used for wiping up all spills, soiling of blood, urine and feces, cleaning of diaper change tables, cleaning of play equipment and toys and cleaning of all the equipment used by children in the preschool area.

6. All infant and toddler toys and all play equipment in the preschool area shall be cleaned with the disinfecting solution after each session. All equipment in infant and toddler rooms (e.g., cribs, swings, walkers) shall be wiped thoroughly with the disinfecting solution after each session.

7. All diaper and trash contaminated with spills of blood, urine and feces shall be placed in trash cans that are lined with disposable plastic liners and are covered and out of reach of children.

## References

AIDS Policy, Millington Baptist Church, Basking Ridge, New Jersey, June 1988.

Amos, William E. *Enabling the Church to Respond*, Chapter 6, "When AIDS Comes to Church," Westminster Press, 1988.

Excerpts from Publications of the National Association of Church Business Administration.

Infection Control Policies, Physician's Clinic, Omaha, Nebraska.

*Pediatric Guidelines for Infection Control of Human Immunodeficiency Virus (Acquired Immunodeficiency Virus) in Hospitals, Medical Offices, Schools and Other Settings.* Section, "Guidelines for Infection Control in Day-Care Centers". Task Forces on Pediatric AIDS, Pediatrics (Professional Publication of American Academy of Pediatrics), November 1988.

"Prevention, Control and Management of Infections in Day Care." In *Health in Day Care: A Manual for Health Professionals.* American Academy of Pediatrics, 1987.

*Rules and Regulations for Day-Care Centers,* Georgia Department of Human Resources.

Used by permission.

# Infection Control Procedures
## *Christ Community Church*

1. Wear disposable gloves when
   a. Accompanying a child to the toilet.
   b. Changing diapers.
   c. In potential contact with blood (i.e., nosebleed).

   Change gloves between each new child contact.

   If an emergency precludes use of gloves when in contact with blood, thoroughly wash with soap and water.

2. Change diapers on disposable wax paper sheets. Dispose of diaper, gloves and wax paper sheets in covered trash container.

3. Wash hands (antiseptic wipe is OK)
   a. After accompanying a child to the toilet.
   b. After changing a diaper.
   c. After assisting a child with wiping his or her nose.
   d. Before food preparation.

4. Have child wash hands
   a. After toileting.
   b. After contact with nasal secretions.
   c. Before eating (antiseptic wipe is OK).

   Use only disposable towels.

5. Disinfect toy if child is seen to put it in his mouth.

6. Use disinfecting solution to
   a. Wipe spills.
   b. Clean diaper changing tables.
   c. Clean soiling from blood, urine or feces.
   d. Clean all equipment after each session.

7. Place the following in covered trash cans:
   a. Diapers.

b. Trash contaminated with blood, urine or feces.

c. Used rubber gloves.

Used by permission.

# AIDS/Communicable Disease Policy
## *Lombard Bible Church*

As Christians, we believe the Bible to be the ultimate authority for our beliefs and behavior. The AIDS epidemic is a call to our members and all of society to return to obedience to the teachings of Scripture. We also believe it is an opportunity to reach out to those who have been infected with this disease because of sinful conduct, as well as to those who have been the innocent victims of others' destructive behavior.

Our goal is to help both groups of sufferers understand that Christ invites all to come to Him for forgiveness and acceptance. This policy has been written with the hope that Christ's love will be thoughtfully demonstrated in the church.

1. Acquired Immune Deficiency Syndrome (AIDS) is an infection caused by the Human Immunodeficiency Virus (HIV). This virus greatly reduces or sometimes destroys the body's immune system. The immune system is the body's defense system and is responsible for fighting disease. Because the immune system is weakened, infections that are normally harmless to a healthy person can be dangerous or even fatal to a person with AIDS. These normally harmless infections are called opportunistic infections.

    According to the most recent research published by the Institute of Medicine, the National Academy of Sciences and the American Red Cross, the AIDS virus spreads through infected persons to others by sexual intercourse, direct blood transfer and intravenous drug use (IV). The virus also can be passed on from infected mothers to their babies during pregnancy, at birth or shortly after birth.

2. While all persons who wish to participate with us at Lombard Bible Church will certainly be welcomed, we have instituted precautions to minimize the risk of the spread of communicable diseases.

    a. We ask that potential workers who have communicable diseases not apply to work or volunteer to work in our facilities while diagnosed as "communicable" by a physician. Workers, while employed or active as volunteers, should let their supervisors know immediately when they are so diagnosed and shall refrain from working in the facility during the period of communicability.

b. We ask parents to be careful with their children when exposed to any communicable disease and to keep their children out of our care facilities if diagnosed or suspected of carrying a communicable disease. We also need to ask parents to inform us if their children inadvertently may have exposed other children to a communicable disease while in our care.

c. Workers in our care facilities should follow the commonly accepted guidelines for the prevention of any infection.

**Precautions**

Use good hygiene to prevent the spread of any communicable disease.

i. Wash hands with soap and warm water before preparing, serving or eating food; after toileting, diaper changes or assists; after sneezing or nose wiping; and after cleaning up body fluids.

ii. Wash toys, equipment, clothes, linens or surfaces exposed to body fluids with a disinfectant.

iii. It is suggested that vinyl gloves (available in the nursery) be used when handling body fluids, especially if hands are chapped or there are breaks in the skin.

iv. Cover breaks in the skin with Band-Aids.

v. When diapering, use disposable diapers, disposable wipes and dispose of in closed disposable bags.

d. Specifically addressing the AIDS/HIV infected child:

**Nursery**

Because young children from birth until they are toilet-trained often bite, share bottles and pacifiers and require diaper changing, those children who have tested positive for HIV may not be permitted in the nursery. Decisions will be made on a case-by-case basis. Every effort will be made to care for the infants in the church setting.

**Children's Programs**

i. Children who test positive for HIV and who are toilet-trained are welcome to attend Sunday school and all church functions and are encouraged to participate fully. They may have access to the bathroom, drinking fountains and other church facilities.

ii. HIV-positive children who lack control over bodily functions, have open wounds or cuts or display behavior such as biting, may be screened and temporarily excluded.

iii. Parents of all children who attend Lombard Bible Church are asked to keep their children home if they have a contagious illness. This will prevent the spread of disease to all children, especially the child with AIDS.

## Summary and Conclusions

We believe that responses to AIDS and other infectious diseases will change as circumstances change. This policy will be reviewed and updated as needed.

We believe that the AIDS epidemic is not only a medical crisis and a national public health emergency, it is also a spiritual challenge.

We believe that issues of life and death, and proclaiming life in the face of death, have always been primary for the church. To help someone die in circumstances that surround him/her with loving support is a challenge that is already part of the ministry of the church. Our ministry with the dying is, without question, one that should be extended to the person with AIDS. In whatever ways we minister to persons with AIDS or other diseases, we need to remember that we are called upon to do more than help the HIV-infected person die well. We are called upon to witness about Jesus Christ, who proclaimed life even in the midst of death. Christ gave His life so that all who believe in Him might be renewed into fellowship with God. We witness to this relationship through our actions to bind up wounds, to sit at bedsides and listen without fear or judgment and to bring this message to those who are suffering.

Submitted by the Christian Education Committee with consultation of Elders.

Used by permission.

# A Statement from the Elders on HIV (the AIDS Virus) and Our Church's Response to Those Infected
### *Grace Church*

We believe that it is the responsibility of Grace Church to encourage righteousness in the way that we individually and corporately demonstrate the breadth and length and height and depth of Christ's love to all of God's creation (Ephesians 3:14-19). Because of the presence of growing numbers of persons with Acquired Immune Deficiency Syndrome (AIDS) in our society and the fears that many have about having casual contact with such persons, the Elder Leadership Team of Grace Church has adopted the following policy on AIDS to apply to all aspects of the life of the church.

Regardless of the factors that may have led to the contracting of a particular disease, Christians are called to have compassion on all persons in need. As followers of Jesus Christ, we must follow His example and teaching, as well as those of the Old and New Testament writers, in showing comfort and compassion to those who suffer from AIDS or are HIV-positive. Just as Jesus showed compassion on those with leprosy (the AIDS of His day), so we must show concern, compassion and Christ's love, and attempt to comfort those who may have this equally dreaded disease of our day and society. Colossians 3:12 urges us as God's chosen ones to be full of compassion, kindness and gentleness to those afflicted persons around us.

Acquired Immune Deficiency Syndrome (AIDS) is a serious, life-threatening condition that is not transmissible by casual contact. The best scientific evidence indicates that AIDS is caused by a virus known as HIV (human immunodeficiency virus), which is transmitted through the exchange of blood or semen by infected sexual partners, contaminated needles, contaminated blood or by infected mothers to their infants.

Medical knowledge about AIDS is developing, and thus is incomplete. It is almost certainly true that infection with the HIV virus takes a multiplicity of forms, some disabling and some not, varying not only from individual to individual, but also from one phase to another within the same individual. From what is known today, AIDS reduces the body's immune response, leaving the infected person vulnerable to life-threatening infections and malignancies.

In responding to the knowledge that someone attending Grace Church has been infected with the AIDS virus, the Elders will be guided by current medical knowledge, the known behavior of Jesus Christ and the principles of compassion and ministry established in the Bible.

An individual who has been diagnosed as being HIV-positive or who has AIDS will be treated with the same compassion as any other individual attending Grace Church. In general, Grace Church will not reject or ostracize anyone who is HIV-positive or who has AIDS as long as that individual presents no real threat to the safety of others in the congregation. The confidentiality of HIV-positive individuals will be determined on a case-by-case basis considering the risk of potential exposure of others within the church.

No child known to be infected with HIV will be excluded from any service, class or social function of the church, except in the case of children with open skin lesions (i.e., cuts, scrapes, sores), and then only temporarily. In the case of infants and toddlers, the HIV-infected child will be integrated into the child care ministry of the church on a case-by-case basis in a manner appropriate to the child's individual situation and consistent with U.S. Public Health Services guidelines, and will always receive one-on-one supervision while they are a participant in the nursery program. All child care providers in the ministries of Grace Church will receive appropriate training.

We acknowledge that there are innocent victims who contract AIDS through no fault of their own, such as health care workers, those who contract HIV through blood transfusions, rape and babies born to HIV-positive mothers. However, due to the fact that AIDS has been spread in our nation and world primarily through behavior that is immoral (sexual immorality) and/or illegal (drug abuse), we must affirm the biblical teaching that sexual intimacy is to be experienced only in the committed relationship of heterosexual marriage. Other kinds of sexual behavior are not only dishonoring to God but bear specific consequences of spiritual guilt and physical disease.

We believe that issues of life and death, and proclaiming life in the face of death, are always primary for the church. Thus, we proclaim to all persons, including the person with AIDS, God's free gift of forgiveness and eternal life, and we choose to demonstrate the power of God's love through our actions to bind up wounds and to sit at bedsides and listen without fear or judgment.

Finally, we believe that responses to AIDS will change as circumstances change or as new information concerning the disease is known. Therefore, this policy will be reviewed and updated as necessary.

Approved 6/20/99

Used by permission.

# Policy on AIDS
## *Westmont Alliance Church*

## A. Medical Facts

Acquired Immunodeficiency Syndrome (AIDS) caused by the Human Immunodeficiency Virus (HIV) is an infectious disease for which there is no known cure. Persons who develop the full spectrum of the disease become tragically ill and invariably die. A person may be infected with the virus for up to 10 years without symptoms. During this time, the person is contagious but may be totally unaware of the infection. It has become a significant problem in our country as well as in the rest of the world. According to current medical knowledge, the Human Immunodeficiency Virus is not highly contagious by casual contact. It is not transmitted through a kiss, hug or handshake, nor is it transmitted by mosquitoes or via toilet seats. However, it is highly transmissible in the following ways:

1. Sexual intercourse, both homosexual and heterosexual, with an infected individual.
2. Use of contaminated needles or other instruments, especially as in intravenous drug use.
3. Blood transfusions of infected blood, blood products and clotting factors (for hemophiliacs), especially prior to 1983 when such products were not screened for the HIV virus.
4. Intrauterine transfer from an infected mother to an unborn infant.

## B. Scriptural Principles

1. Biblical Sexuality

    As Christians we believe the Bible to be authoritative for faith and practice. Therefore, we accept all Scripture and biblical principles to be authoritative in relation to human sexuality and the proper care of our bodies. We hold as unacceptable behavior the following practices:

    a. All homosexuality (Romans 1:24-27).
    b. Heterosexual relations (as relating to a man and a woman) outside of marriage (1 Corinthians 6:19).
    c. Drug abuse (1 Corinthians 3:16-17).

We affirm our belief in:

    a. Heterosexual marriage (Genesis 2:24).

b. Abstinence outside such a marriage (1 Corinthians 6:13–18).

c. Faithfulness to one's spouse (Hebrews 13:4).

d. The body as the temple of the Holy Spirit (1 Corinthians 6:19).

2. Christian Ministry

As Christians we believe we are called to be God's ambassadors of the good news as well as agents of helping and healing to our world (Matthew 25:34-40). We believe that we should love and minister to people regardless of their behavior or circumstances. While we correctly judge heterosexual intercourse outside marriage and all homosexual intercourse as sin, we advocate that Christians refrain from cultivating a judgmental spirit. Whether an individual has contracted AIDS through a sinful lifestyle or by another means, we believe that ostracism, censoriousness, avoidance or desertion are wholly unacceptable Christian responses. Our response will be one of compassion and inclusion. We resolve to follow the example of the Lord, who willingly crossed barriers, touched lepers, accepted risks and identified with all people.

## C. Policies

1. Westmont Alliance Church desires to establish policies and procedures that will fulfill the following three priorities:

a. As a Christ-centered, compassionate church, we wish to offer support, caring and an opportunity to worship to all people, including those who are infected with HIV.

b. We desire to protect those infected with HIV from additional infectious diseases.

c. We desire to protect the uninfected church attendees from undue risk of contracting the virus.

2. To these ends, we have established the following policies. Procedural guidelines will also be drawn up to help in the implementation of these policies.

a. AIDS Council

A council made up primarily of the elders, but including the Christian education chairman and Sunday school superintendent, will consult with physicians and lawyers as they deem necessary.

b. Confidentiality

The church leadership (i.e., pastoral staff and elders) will maintain confidentiality about an individual who tests positive for HIV, unless the individual is engaged in behavior that is putting others at risk. Any person who persists in dangerous or unbiblical behavior will come under the discipline of the church.

c. Nursery

Because young children from birth until they are toilet-trained often bite, share bottles and pacifiers and require diaper changing, those children who have tested positive for HIV might not be permitted in the nursery. Decisions will be made on a case-by-case basis. Every effort will be made to care for the infants in the church setting.

d. Children's Programs

i. Children who test positive for HIV and who are toilet-trained are welcome to attend Sunday school and all church functions and are encouraged to participate fully. They may have access to bathrooms, drinking fountains and other church facilities.

ii. HIV-positive children who lack control over bodily functions, have open wounds or cuts or display behavior such as biting, may be screened and temporarily excluded. This decision will be made by the AIDS Council.

iii. Parents of all children who attend Westmont Alliance Church are asked to keep their children home if they have a contagious illness. This will prevent the spread of disease to all children, especially the child with AIDS.

e. Adult Program

Adults who are HIV-positive are warmly welcomed into our congregation, and they should expect to be treated with Christian love and care. This does not diminish our stand regarding unbiblical sexual behavior or drug use. Adults who test HIV-positive may be asked to refrain from certain areas of service. Each case will be decided by the AIDS Council.

f. Premarital Testing

The pastoral staff and elders of the church retain the right to require testing for HIV in persons seeking to be married at Westmont Alliance Church who are deemed high risk for AIDS. This is to protect the potential partner of such a marriage.

g.  Education

Westmont Alliance Church is committed to teaching the sanctity of monogamous heterosexual marriage and the dangers of sexual immorality. We will assist the parents in the instruction of their children and continue sex education programs already in the Christian education curriculum, including information regarding AIDS and HIV infections.

h.  Ministry to Those with AIDS

As need grows within the congregation and community, Westmont Alliance Church is committed to ministering specifically to people who are affected by AIDS.

Used by permission.

# Policy on AIDS—Section A—Guidelines
## *Westgate Chapel*

It is our intention as a church not to discriminate against any person with AIDS. We desire to avoid reactions based upon exaggerated fears and prejudice. We do, however, have the responsibility to protect the health and safety of both our staff and those who attend The Chapel.

After a thorough review of current medical research and in consultation with Christian health professionals, we have established the following guidelines:

1. Those parents bringing an infant (still in diapers) for the first time will be asked to fill out a registration card that includes a question as to whether the infant has tested HIV-positive.

2. Children under the age of four who have tested HIV-positive are welcome at The Chapel and will be cared for in a special, isolated care facility. Their parents also may keep these children with them as they attend services. Children who are above the age of four and are toilet-trained will be mainstreamed.

3. When a child is known to have tested HIV-positive, the teachers and staff directly involved with that child will be informed of the child's condition.

4. No adult who is HIV-positive can be involved in food preparation or serving of any kind.

5. Parents who have a child/youth through grade 12 who has tested HIV-positive must indicate so on the registration form (when applicable before their child participates in extracurricular activities that could involve risk).

6. Adults who have tested HIV-positive must indicate on the registration form (when applicable) before they may participate in extracurricular activities that could involve risk.

(PLEASE NOTE: In some states it is illegal to ask for personal information such as that listed in the points above. Before asking questions of a personal nature, be sure to check with your state laws concerning personal disclosure.)

# Policy on AIDS—Section B—
# Procedures for Handling Blood and Body Spills
## *Westgate Chapel*

The Center for Disease Control (CDC) has established a set of standard precautions for handling spills of blood or bodily fluids to minimize the risk of the spread of communicable diseases. These will be adapted for The Chapel nursery and child-care areas as outlined below.

These guidelines are to be followed by any worker with actual or potential exposure to a child's blood or body fluids. Body fluids include saliva, sputum, urine, fecal material, nasal discharge and discharge from open skin sores, sweat and tears.

1. Gloves must be worn for touching blood and body fluids, mucous membranes (eye/nose/mouth) or non-intact skin (cuts, open sores), and for handling items or surfaces soiled with blood or body fluids. Gloves should be changed after each contact.

2. Hands and other skin surfaces should be washed immediately and thoroughly if exposed to blood or body fluids. Hands should be washed immediately after gloves are removed. Careful handwashing after each contact is essential to prevent spread of infection.

3. Cleaning of body fluids on any surface shall be done with gloves. The surface on which a spill occurred (on which a child was changed if a nonporous barrier was not used) shall be cleaned with SLUFF (available from our maintenance department). Where possible, the use of nonporous barriers is encouraged to simplify cleanup after changing diapers. The use of such barriers does not negate the responsibility of the worker to ensure that proper cleanup of inadvertent spillage has been done.

4. No worker who has an exudative or weeping skin sore shall handle any situation involving potential blood/body fluid contact.

5. All contaminated cleanup materials shall be disposed of in sealed plastic trash bags placed in a larger trash bag out of the reach of children.

6. All wounds must be covered on workers and children.

7. Toys soiled by saliva ideally should never be shared and at minimum should be washed in SLUFF after each use.

8. Toileting of children with poor personal hygiene should be done by an adult wearing gloves. Gloves should be disposed of immediately.

Used by permission.

# TRAINING MINISTRY VOLUNTEERS

Regardless of position, title or time commitment, all screened and approved volunteers should receive training prior to being placed in a ministry position. Training should include all employees, pastoral staff, day care workers, etc., and ministry volunteers—leaders, teachers and workers. Such individuals need to know and agree to the standards, policies and procedures established and enforced by the respective church or ministry organization. Intentional, quality training will go a long way in preventing an individual from claiming ignorance or putting the church, its volunteers and its children, youth and adults at risk.

As a minimum, initial training should include the following for every leader, teacher and worker:

- Presentation and completion of the "Points to Ponder" worksheets provided in chapter 8.
- A verbal review of the printed copy of the church's Safe Place Plan. Each trainee should have a hard copy.
- A signed statement indicating that the individual has read, understands and agrees with the Safe Place Plan. (See volunteer personnel form in Appendix A.)

## INITIAL TRAINING

Your Safe Place Plan needs to be well explained. It is important that the volunteers understand your policies and procedures so that they can comply with, support and follow the plan. The "Creating a Safe Place—Points to Ponder" worksheets found in chapter 8 have been designed to assist you with this initial training. For easy reproduction, worksheet outlines are also available on the CD located inside the back cover of this book. The "Creating a Safe Place—Points to Ponder" worksheets may be reproduced for local church and organizational purposes but not for commercial use or resale.

## Continuing Education

Additional training and ongoing awareness should be periodically offered to volunteers. Some suggestions for continuing education are listed below.

- Recognizing clues of neglect and physical abuse
  See Appendix S, "Recognizing Signs of Abuse." Also refer to page 38 of manual.
  Contact your state's Department of Health and Human Services or child protection services agency for information.

- Blood-borne pathogen/standard precaution policies
  An excellent source of information for understanding the issues and formulating a plan is *Legal Legislative Update*, February 1994, Vol. 4, Issue 3, Association of Christian Schools International. (An article from this issue entitled "Responding to OSHA's Final Rule for 'Occupational Exposure to Blood-Borne Pathogens' " is available in Appendix L. Also see Appendix M for the "Excerpt from: 'Clarification of the Standard on Occupation Exposure to Blood-Borne Pathogens, 29 CFR 1910.1030.)

- CPR and first aid
  Contact the American Red Cross for training information. Many volunteers may already have CPR certification. Keep current files of those who are certified. You may also want to encourage those who are not certified to go for their CPR certification.

- Emergency procedures and escape routes (fire, tornado, etc.)
  Share your written plan and exit maps/diagrams with leaders.

- Discipline policies/classroom management

- Event procedures

- Circulate pertinent newspaper clippings, magazine articles, etc.

- Check out appropriate Web sites as listed in the bibliography and resources section and elsewhere throughout this book.

Records should be kept of each volunteer's attendance at training events. (See Appendix E for a sample volunteer application approval process form.) Additional continuing education ideas may be found in the bibliography and resources section of this manual.

# CREATING A SAFE PLACE—
# POINTS TO PONDER

## (Reproducible Worksheets/Leader's Guides)

### BEFORE YOU TEACH:

- The following worksheet outlines are taken directly from the Training Points identified throughout the text of this manual.

- Leaders will need to review each designated section to decide what and how much they want to communicate about each point. Leaders should share personal notes and illustrations to add clarity and a personal touch to the presentation.

- To assist the leader, the following outlines contain the corresponding page numbers for each "Point to Ponder."

- The reproducible student worksheets (available on the CD provided inside the back cover) do not include the corresponding page numbers found on the Worksheets/Leader's Guides.

- Leaders will want to refer back to each section they select to review the suggested interactive Training Tips so that they can integrate them into their presentations.

- Leaders should be sure to refer to the pre-session Training Tips located in the introduction for fun ways to introduce the training session.

# UNDERSTANDING THE ISSUES

## A. UNDERSTANDING THE NEED [PP. 5-7]

_____

_____

_____

_____

_____

_____

_____

_____

_____

_____

## B. UNDERSTANDING CHILD ABUSE [PP. 7-8]

1. Definition of Child Abuse: _____

_____

_____

2. Four Categories of Abuse

   a. _____

   b. _____

c. _____

d. _____

3.  Neglect

a.  Physical _____

_____

_____

b.  Emotional _____

_____

_____

4.  Adults, Elderly and People with Disabilities _____

_____

_____

_____

## C. UNDERSTANDING THE CHURCH'S RESPONSIBILITY [PP. 8-10]

1.  Scriptural and Moral Responsibility

a. _____

b. _____

c. _____

d. _____

e. _____

f. _____

g. _____

# "What did you do to prevent this tragedy from happening?"

2.  Civil and Legal Liability _____

_____

_____

_____

_____

_____

_____

_____

_____

_____

_____

# RECRUITING MINISTRY VOLUNTEERS

## A. COMMITTEE/BOARD APPROVAL [P. 12]

_____

_____

_____

_____

_____

_____

_____

## B. VOLUNTEER PERSONNEL FORM [P. 12]

(Be sure to go through a copy of the form found in Appendix A.)

_____

_____

_____

_____

_____

_____

_____

# CREATING A SAFE ENVIRONMENT

## A. STAFFING AND SUPERVISING [PP. 15-16]

1. Two-Adult Rule

2. Open Doors

3. Family Protection

4. Teacher/Student Ratios

5. Volunteer Age

6. Supervision

_____

_____

_____

## B. EARLY CHILDHOOD/ELEMENTARY CONSIDERATIONS [PP. 16-19]

1. Volunteer Identification

_____

_____

_____

2. Child Registration

_____

_____

_____

3. Volunteer Registration

_____

_____

_____

4. Releasing Children

_____

_____

_____

5. Diaper Changing

_____

_____

_____

6.  Rest Room Guidelines _____

_____

_____

7.  Clean Hands _____

_____

_____

## C. Health and Safety Guidelines [pp. 19-22]

1.  Well Child Policy _____

_____

_____

2.  Medications _____

_____

_____

_____

3.  Emergencies _____

_____

_____

## D. Responding to an Injury or Illness [pp. 22-23]

1.  _____

2.  _____

3.  _____

4. _____

5. _____

6. _____

7. _____

8. _____

## E. HOUSEKEEPING [P. 23]

1. Nursery/Classrooms _____

_____

_____

2. Custodial Cleaning _____

_____

_____

## G. PROPER DISPLAY OF AFFECTION [PP. 24-25]

1. Appropriate Touch

   a. _____

   _____

   b. _____

   _____

   c. _____

   _____

   d. _____

e. _____
_____

f. _____
_____

g. _____
_____

2. Inappropriate Touch

a. _____
_____

b. _____
_____

c. _____
_____

d. _____
_____

e. _____
_____

f. _____
_____

## H. Special Events and Overnight Policies (pp. 26-27)

1. Field Trips, Special Events and Personal Appointments _____

_____

_____

2.  Transportation _____

_____

_____

3.  Overnight Events _____

_____

_____

## I. DISCIPLINE POLICY [PP. 27-28]

1.  Reward _____

_____

_____

2.  Remind _____

_____

_____

3.  Redirect _____

_____

_____

4.  Remove _____

_____

_____

5.  Return _____

_____

_____

6.  Suggested Classroom Manners

   a. _____

   b. _____

   c. _____

   d. _____

   e. _____

# REPORTING PROCEDURES

## A. OBLIGATION TO REPORT [PP. 37-39]

1. Who Must Report

 

 

 

 

2. What to Report

    a.

    b.

    c.

    d.

    e.

    f.

    g.

    h.

    i.

    j.

    k.

    l.

3. Confidentiality _____

_____

_____

_____

_____

4. Responding to the Student _____

_____

_____

_____

_____

5. Report Form _____

_____

_____

_____

_____

6. Summary of Steps

    a. _____

       _____

    b. _____

       _____

    c. _____

       _____

Adams, Caren, M.A., and Jennifer Fay, M.A. *Helping Your Child Recover from Sexual Abuse*. Seattle, WA: University of Washington Press, 1992.

Allender, Dan B., and Larry Crabb. *The Wounded Heart—Hope for Adult Victims of Childhood Sexual Abuse*. Colorado Springs, CO: NavPress, 1990.

Anderson, Bill. *When Child Abuse Comes to Church*. Minneapolis, MN: Bethany, 1992.

Choun, Robert J., and Michael S. Lawson. *The Complete Handbook for Children's Ministry*. Nashville, TN: Thomas Nelson Publishers, 1993.

Crabtree, Jack. *Play It Safe*. Wheaton, IL: Victor Books, 1993.

Kepler, Victoria. *One in Four—Handling Child Sexual Abuse—What Every Professional Should Know*. Mansfield, OH: Social Interest Press, 1984.

Kilborn, Phyllis, and Marjorie McDermind. *Sexually Exploited Children: Working to Protect and Heal*. Monrovia, CA: MARC Publications, 1998.

Zarra, Ernest J. III. *It Should Never Happen Here*. Grand Rapids, MI: Baker Books, 1997.

## WEB SITES:

**www.childsexualabuse.org**: An excellent Web site for articles, policies and trends in dealing with child sexual abuse. Includes links to other child safety sites.

**www.iclonline.com**: For training materials on reducing the risk of child sexual abuse in your church. Available from Christian Ministry Resources, P.O. Box 1098, Matthews, NC 28106, or call 800.222.1840.

**www.calib.com/nccanch**: National Clearinghouse on Child Abuse and Neglect Information. A national resource for professionals and others seeking information on child abuse and neglect and child welfare.

# appendix A

## VOLUNTEER PERSONNEL FORM

---

*Church/Organization Name*

## Application for Work with Children, Youth or Adults

This form is to be completed in ink by any applicant for a volunteer position within/ involving: _____

*Church/Organization Name*

ministry to and with individuals at all age levels. We recognize that this form is extensive, but ask for your patience in completing the form in its entirety. Your cooperation will assist church leaders in their efforts to provide a secure environment for you as a volunteer as well as the children, youth and adults who participate in our ministry programs and use our facilities. Your responses will be maintained confidentially, although there may be circumstances where such information may be provided on a "need to know" basis to individuals working with our ministry and to other individuals in order to evaluate your application and/or to comply with applicable legal requirements.

NOTE: If you live in a state where laws exempt you from providing any of the information requested below, you need not answer the questions requesting such information. For example, you need not disclose information that is contained in sealed or expunged court records, or that involves a criminal arrest that did not result in conviction.

Date: _____

# PERSONAL DATA

Please print:

Name: _____
                    *Last*                          *First*                  *Middle*

If you have ever used other names, please provide complete name(s) and date in use:

_____      _____
                        *Name*                                 *Date*

_____      _____
                        *Name*                                 *Date*

_____      _____
                        *Name*                                 *Date*

Social Security Number: _____ - _____ - _____

Home Phone: (     ) _____

Present Address: _____

_____
                             *Address*

_____
             *City*                   *State*         *Zip*

Date of Birth (if you are under 18 years of age): _____

Marital Status: _____

Previous Address: _____

_____
*Address*

_____
*City*                          *State*            *Zip*

## SPIRITUAL HISTORY

How long have you attended _____ Church?
                                    *Church/Organization Name*

Are you a member of _____ Church? ___ Yes ___ No
                          *Church/Organization Name*

If not, are you willing to attend a membership class? ___ Yes ___ No

Do you attend regularly (two or more services a month)? ___ Yes ___ No

Have you been baptized? ___ Yes ___ No

   In a brief paragraph, please outline your spiritual journey, including when you received Christ as Savior.

_____

_____

_____

_____

_____

Have you taken any courses or received any training that would equip you for Christian ministry? If so, please list.

_____

_____

_____

# MINISTRY HISTORY

Please list the churches you have attended and the ministry organizations in which you have participated within the last five years.

1. Name: _____

   Address: _____

   _____

   Phone: ( ____ ) _____

   Dates Attended: _____

2. Name: _____

   Address: _____

   _____

   Phone: ( ____ ) _____

   Dates Attended: _____

3. Name: _____

   Address: _____

   _____

   Phone: ( ____ ) _____

   Dates Attended: _____

Please list present and previous ministry experience:

|   | Ministry | Pastor/Supervisor Phone |
|---|----------|-------------------------|
| 1. | _____ | ( ) _____ |
| 2. | _____ | ( ) _____ |
| 3. | _____ | ( ) _____ |

## QUALIFICATIONS AND AVAILABILITY FOR SERVICE

Briefly share your motivation for wanting to serve in the ministries of this local church.

_____

_____

_____

_____

_____

On what date would you be available? _____

Describe any condition or limitation that might restrict or prevent you from performing certain activities involved in the volunteer position for which you are being considered (i.e. lifting, handling an emergency, driving, participating in certain sports, etc.).

_____

_____

_____

Do you have a contagious or infectious disease or condition which could be transmitted to others in the volunteer work you would be performing? ____ Yes ____ No  If yes, please explain on the next page.

_____

_____

_____

_____

What type of ministry do you prefer? Please circle all categories that apply.

| AGE LEVEL | MINISTRY INTEREST | MINISTRY PROGRAM |
|---|---|---|
| Nursery (0-2 yrs.) | Teaching | S.S./Bible Teaching |
| Early Childhood (2-5 yrs.) | Teaching Assistant | Children's Church |
| Elementary (6-11 yrs.) | Administration | Club Ministries |
| Youth (12-17/18 yrs.) | Music | Youth or Small Groups |
| College Age | Disabilities Ministries | Outreach |
| Adult | Arts, Crafts | Summer Ministries |
| Senior Adult | Games, Activities/Drama | Other: _____ |

# LEGAL QUESTIONNAIRE

1. Have you ever been convicted of a criminal offense (felony or misdemeanor, except for minor traffic violations)? You will need to answer "Yes" if you have entered into a plea agreement, including a deferred sentence or deferred judgment arrangement, in connection with a criminal charge. ____ Yes ____ No

    If you have been convicted of such an offense, please attach a statement or explanation, including nature of offense, date, court where conviction was entered and any other relevant information.

2. Have you ever been convicted of a sexual offense, offense relating to children or crime of violence (that is not covered in question 1 above)? ____ Yes ____ No

    If you have been convicted of such an offense, please attach a statement or explanation, including nature of offense charged, date, law enforcement agency making the charge and any other relevant information.

3. Have you ever been reported to a social services agency, law enforcement authority, child abuse registry or similar organization regarding abuse or misconduct involving children? ____ Yes ____ No If yes, please explain.

    _____

    _____

    _____

4. Have you had any painful experience (personal abuse in any form) that has better equipped you, or may hinder you from a productive ministry? ____ Yes ____ No If yes, please explain.

    _____

    _____

    _____

5. Have you ever been the subject of a civil lawsuit involving sexual misconduct, sexual harassment or other immoral behavior or conduct, involving adults or children? ____ Yes ____ No  If yes, please explain.

_____

_____

_____

6. Have you ever been the subject of a complaint or disciplinary proceeding against a professional license or other license held by you, including but not limited to a license to provide child care or similar services? ____ Yes ____ No  If yes, please explain.

_____

_____

_____

7. Have you ever been the subject of any disciplinary action, transfer or dismissal, or been named as a defendant in a civil lawsuit, as a result of an accident or mishap involving children? ____ Yes ____ No  If yes, please explain.

_____

_____

_____

8. Have you ever been subject to any disciplinary action (including discharge) or investigation by a church, religious or other organization or by an employer? ____ Yes ____ No  If yes, please explain.

_____

_____

_____

9. Do you have any drug, alcohol or substance abuse problems? ____ Yes ____ No  If yes, please explain.

_____

_____

_____

10. Do you practice a sexually pure lifestyle as taught in the Scriptures? ____ Yes ____ No
**BE ASSURED THAT YOUR COMMENTS WILL BE HELD IN STRICT CONFIDENCE.**

## PERSONAL REFERENCES

1. Name: _____

   Address: _____

   _____

   Phone:  ( ____ ) _____

   Relationship: _____

2. Name: _____

   Address: _____

   _____

   Phone:  ( ____ ) _____

   Relationship: _____

3. Name: _____

   Address: _____

   _____

   Phone:  ( ____ ) _____

   Relationship: _____

It is desirable that all teachers be members of the local church; if they are not, they must be in full harmony with the doctrines and principles of _____.

*Church/Organization Name*

## Applicant's Statement

The responses I have provided in completing this application form are complete, truthful and accurate.

I hereby authorize _____

*Church/Organization Name*

(hereunto referred to as "the Church") to make inquiries concerning my background in connection with evaluating the information I have provided on this form and in the application process, including a criminal records check if deemed necessary by the Church. I hereby authorize all persons associated with me, including churches, employers, law enforcement agencies, licensing and social services agencies, to release any information contained in their files or records concerning me to the Church and its representatives.

In consideration of the receipt and evaluation of this application form by the Church, I hereby release _____

*Church/Organization Name*

and their directors, employees, agents, representatives and any other person or organization, including record custodians, that may release information concerning me, both collectively and individually, from any and all liability for damages of whatever kind or nature which may at any time result to me, my heirs or family on account of inquiries concerning my background and any disclosures of information concerning me to:

_____

*Church/Organization Name*

I waive any right that I may have to inspect any information provided about me by any person or organization identified by me in this application.

I HAVE CAREFULLY READ THE FOREGOING RELEASE AND KNOW THE CONTENTS OF IT, AND I SIGN THIS RELEASE AS MY OWN FREE AND VOLUNTARY ACT.

I understand that my service with the Church shall be volunteer service. In addition, my volunteer services shall be at-will and the Church shall be entitled to terminate my services at any time, with or without cause or advance notice. I understand and agree that I am not an employee of the Church and that I have no expectation of future employment. As a volunteer, I have no entitlement to or expectation of compensation, health insurance or other employee benefits, or unemployment or worker's compensation insurance benefits.

I affirm that I will strictly comply with all policies and procedures of:

_____

*Church/Organization Name*

including but not limited to its Safe Place Plan. If at any time I find that for any reason I am unable to support the vision, policies, procedures or doctrine of this church/organization, I will resign my volunteer position. I understand and agree that failure by me to abide by such policies and procedures may result in my immediate dismissal, or in disciplinary action, all at the discretion of the Church. I will report any known or suspected child abuse or other violation of policy to the senior pastor, a member of church staff, an elder or the designated authority.

Applicant's Signature: _____ Date: _____

Applicant's Name (please print): _____

Witness' Signature: _____ Date: _____

Witness' Name (please print): _____

## REFERENCE CHECK RECORD

*Church/Organization Name*

## Record of Contact with References and Churches/ Organizations Identified by a Volunteer Applicant

Name of Applicant: _____

### REFERENCES

### Church/Organization

Church/Organization Contacted: _____

Date: _____ Method of contact: ○ phone ○ letter ○ interview

Person making contact: _____

Summary of contact: _____

_____

_____

_____

Did the reference refuse to provide information? ____ Yes ____ No

## Business/Person

Business/Person Contacted: _____

Date: _____  Method of contact:  ○ phone  ○ letter  ○ interview

Person making contact: _____

Summary of contact: _____

_____

_____

_____

Did the reference refuse to provide information? ____ Yes ____ No

## Business/Person

Business/Person Contacted: _____

Date: _____  Method of contact:  ○ phone  ○ letter  ○ interview

Person making contact: _____

Summary of contact: _____

_____

_____

_____

Did the reference refuse to provide information? ____ Yes ____ No

## SCREENING VOLUNTEERS

---

*Church/Organization Name*

## Telephone Script

### WHEN CALLING A VOLUNTEER'S FORMER CHURCH

"Hello, this is _____ . I serve on the Christian Education

Board of _____ in _____ .

Like many churches today, we have a screening policy for everyone who volunteers to

work in church ministries. I am calling you because . . .

_____ indicated that he/she:

*Name of Applicant*

- attended your church in _____ year;

- became a member in _____ year; or

- volunteered as a _____ in _____

  department from _____ to _____

Can you verify this information? ____ Yes ____ No

Would you have any reservations about recommending _____

for work in our church ministry programs? ____ Yes ____ No

Thank you very much for your help."

## WHEN CALLING A BUSINESS OR PERSONAL REFERENCE

"Hello, this is _____ . I serve on the Christian Education

Board of _____ in _____ .

Like many churches today, we have a screening policy for everyone who volunteers to

work in church ministries. I am calling you because . . .

_____ listed you as a personal reference.

*Name of Applicant*

How do you know _____ ?

Would you have any reservations about _____

*Name of Applicant*

working with _____ (children, youth or adult—identify

which age level applicant will be working with)? ____ Yes ____ No

Thank you very much for your help."

NOTE: Record all comments, including any reservations, in the summary of contact section provided on the reference portion of the volunteer form.

## REFERENCE RESPONSE INFORMATION

_____

*Church/Organization Name*

To: _____

From: _____

*Name of Ministry*

Address: _____

_____

Regarding: _____

*Name of Worker Candidate*

To Whom It May Concern:

The above-mentioned individual, who has expressed an interest in working with (identify age-level) in our ministry, has listed you as a reference. In order for our organization to properly evaluate the qualifications of this worker candidate, we would like you to complete this form with your honest opinions and impressions of the candidate. The above-mentioned individual will not have access to your responses.

Please complete the following form in ink and return it to our organization in the enclosed stamped, self-addressed envelope. Thank you for your assistance in this regard.

1. How long have you known the above-mentioned individual? _____

_____

2. In what capacity have you come to know this individual (i.e. coworker, neighbor, friend, etc.)? _____

SAFE PLACE

3. In your opinion, is the above-mentioned worker candidate fully qualified to work with (identify age-level)? ____ Yes ____ No  If no, please explain below.

_____

_____

_____

4. What concerns, if any, would you have in allowing this individual to work with children or youth? _____

_____

_____

5. Are you aware of anything in the volunteer's background, personality or behavior that could in any way pose a threat to (identify age-level)? ____ Yes ____ No  If yes, please explain below.

_____

_____

_____

Additional Comments or Explanation:

_____

_____

_____

Thank you for taking the time to complete this form. If you have any questions regarding this form or prefer to speak with someone personally about this reference, please call our church office at:  (        ) _____

Signature: _____  Date: _____

Print Name: _____  Phone:  (        ) _____

Please return this form at your earliest convenience to: _____

# appendix E

## VOLUNTEER APPLICATION
## APPROVAL PROCESS FORM

*Church/Organization Name*
**For Office Use Only**

Name of Volunteer: _____

Ministry Area: _____

1. Reference checks (date completed): _____

2. Government records check (date completed): _____

3. Interview date: _____ Name of Interviewer: _____

4. Initial Safe Place Plan Training (date completed): _____

5. Continued Training

   Topic/Subject: _____ Date: _____

   Topic/Subject: _____ Date: _____

   Topic/Subject: _____ Date: _____

   Topic/Subject: _____ Date: _____

**\* CONFIDENTIAL \***

SAFE

PLACE

101

# appendix F

## CHILD CARE SIGN-IN FORM

### Please complete this information *every time* you bring your child to this room.

Room: _____                    Date: _____

Child's Name: _____    Age: _____

Parent/Guardian: _____    Nursery #: _____

Parent's Location:  S.S.: _____    Sun. a.m.: _____

                     Sun. p.m.: _____    Wed.: _____

Special Instructions: _____

_____

Child's Name: _____    Age: _____

Parent/Guardian: _____    Nursery #: _____

Parent's Location:  S.S.: _____    Sun. a.m.: _____

                     Sun. p.m.: _____    Wed.: _____

Special Instructions: _____

_____

Child's Name: _____ Age: _____

Parent/Guardian: _____ Nursery #: _____

Parent's Location:  S.S.: _____ Sun. a.m.: _____

                Sun. p.m.: _____ Wed.: _____

Special Instructions: _____

_____

---

Child's Name: _____ Age: _____

Parent/Guardian: _____ Nursery #: _____

Parent's Location:  S.S.: _____ Sun. a.m.: _____

                Sun. p.m.: _____ Wed.: _____

Special Instructions: _____

_____

---

Child's Name: _____ Age: _____

Parent/Guardian: _____ Nursery #: _____

Parent's Location:  S.S.: _____ Sun. a.m.: _____

                Sun. p.m.: _____ Wed.: _____

Special Instructions: _____

_____

# appendix G

## VOLUNTEER SIGN-IN SHEET

_____

*Church/Organization Name*

All volunteers are required to sign in upon arrival. Be sure to include classroom, date, name and time. If you leave the room for any reason, please note the time out and the time in again, if applicable. When your scheduled classroom responsibility is completed, please record the time as time out.

| Classroom: _____ | Classroom: _____ |
| Date: _____ | Date: _____ |
| mo./day/yr. | mo./day/yr. |
| Name: _____ | Name: _____ |
| TIME IN: _____ | TIME IN: _____ |
| Time Out: _____ | Time Out: _____ |
| Time In: _____ | Time In: _____ |
| TIME OUT: _____ | TIME OUT: _____ |

| Classroom: | | Classroom: | |
|---|---|---|---|
| Date: | | Date: | |
| | mo./day/yr. | | mo./day/yr. |
| Name: | | Name: | |
| TIME IN: | | TIME IN: | |
| Time Out: | | Time Out: | |
| Time In: | | Time In: | |
| TIME OUT: | | TIME OUT: | |

| Classroom: | | Classroom: | |
|---|---|---|---|
| Date: | | Date: | |
| | mo./day/yr. | | mo./day/yr. |
| Name: | | Name: | |
| TIME IN: | | TIME IN: | |
| Time Out: | | Time Out: | |
| Time In: | | Time In: | |
| TIME OUT: | | TIME OUT: | |

# Diaper-Changing Procedure

1. Wash your hands.
2. Put on gloves.
3. Place clean paper towel on changing pad.
4. Place baby on changing pad.
5. Remove soiled diaper and place in plastic bag.
6. Clean diaper area with wipes.
7. Put wipes in plastic bag.
8. Follow parents' instructions (as per doctor's written order) regarding care of diaper area (powder, ointment, etc.).
9. Put clean diaper on baby.
10. Have another nursery volunteer remove baby from changing area.
11. Remove paper towel from changing pad and put in plastic bag.
12. Remove gloves without touching the exterior surfaces and put in plastic bag.
13. Dispose of plastic bag in trash.
14. Wash your hands.

**NOTE: Each diaper change requires a new pair of gloves.**

# PLEASE WASH YOUR HANDS!

- Use warm running water.

- Use soap!

- Rub hands together to make lather.

- Wash fronts, backs and between fingers.

- Wash for at least 20 seconds.

- Dry hands with a disposable towel.

- Turn off faucet with the towel.

- Dispose of towel in appropriate receptacle.

## WELL CHILD POLICY

## Health Criteria for Children's Ministries

The following list of symptoms will determine if a child should *not* be admitted to our nurseries and classrooms:

- Persistent coughing
- Persistent sneezing
- Any discolored nasal discharge
- Vomiting
- Inflamed throat
- Earaches
- Diarrhea (two or more loose bowel movements)

- Fever (over 99°; must be fever free for 24 hours)
- Runny nose and/or eyes
- Unusual fatigue and irritability
- Complaints of stomachache
- Swollen glands
- Rash (except diaper rash)

If a child shows signs of any of these symptoms while in our care, the child will be isolated from the others and parent or guardian will be contacted. (In the case of children with allergies who might exhibit some of the above-mentioned symptoms, exceptions will be made.)

Our desire is to protect all children and volunteers from exposure to illness. We appreciate your cooperation in maintaining a healthy ministry environment.

# appendix H

# ACCIDENT AND INJURY REPORT FORM

*Church/Organization Name*

## PERSON INJURED

Name: _____ Age/D.O.B.: _____

Address: _____

_____

Phone: ( ) _____

Name of parent(s)/guardian(s) (if person injured is a minor):

_____

Employer: _____

Does the injured party have medical insurance? _____ Yes _____ No

Name of medical insurance company: _____

Injured's relationship to the organization: _____ Member _____ Visitor

_____ Volunteer _____ Employee _____ Student _____ Other

For what purpose was the injured on the premises? _____

_____

_____

_____

## Injury Incident

Date of Injury: _____ Time: _____

Describe the nature and location of injury on body: _____

_____

_____

Describe how the injury happened and where it occurred: _____

_____

_____

Who was responsible for supervision at the time of injury? _____

_____

## Witnesses

Were there other children and/or adults involved? _____ Yes _____ No  If yes, how?

_____

Name of Witness: _____ Phone: ( )_____

Address: _____

Name of Witness: _____ Phone: ( )_____

Address: _____

# Response

How and when was a parent/guardian notified? _____

_____

_____

Were medical personnel consulted or notified? _____ Yes _____ No

If yes, note name, qualifications and treatment given, if any. _____

_____

_____

Was the injured taken to the hospital? _____ Yes _____ No

Hospital Name: _____

If yes, explain why, and who transported. _____

_____

_____

Signature: _____ Date of Report: _____

Church: _____ Position: _____

# appendix L

# RESPONDING TO OSHA'S FINAL RULE FOR "OCCUPATIONAL EXPOSURE TO BLOOD-BORNE PATHOGENS"

## Introduction

Although there are many types of blood-borne pathogens (any microorganism or virus that can cause disease), medical officials are expressing greatest concern about the HIV virus which causes AIDS and the HBV virus which causes hepatitis B. The June 1992 issue of this newsletter featured a four-page article regarding what school personnel needed to know about the HIV virus and AIDS. Included with the medical information were specific recommendations regarding school admission of infected students, extensive guidelines for handling body fluids at school, and information on training the staff in the use of "standard precautions." HIV is a blood-borne, not an air-borne, virus. It may be spread through blood or blood products. HIV is not transmitted through casual contact such as occurs at school. If you do not have a copy of those recommendations, see the Resource List at the end of this article for information on how to obtain it.

The blood-borne virus that an employee is most apt to encounter in a school setting is the HBV virus. It causes hepatitis B, which is up to 100 times more contagious than the HIV virus. In a recent year, more than 200 health care workers died when they were exposed to the HBV virus compared to a very small number who died of AIDS from on-the-job exposure. While the HIV virus usually dies within hours of exposure to air, the HBV virus can live for up to seven days on air-exposed surfaces such as dried blood. One source estimated that there are more than 300,000 new hepatitis B cases nationwide each year. One million people are estimated to be HBV carriers in the United States. While HBV can result in a mild flu-like illness in its early stage, many individuals have few or no noticeable symptoms indicating that they have been exposed to the HBV virus. Later stages of the disease cause liver damage such as cirrhosis, liver cancer, and death due to liver failure. More than 5,000 people die each year from hepatitis B-related illnesses. There is no cure for hepatitis B, but there is a vaccine that has an estimated 90% prevention rate.

## New OSHA Rule

The Occupational Safety and Health Administration's (OSHA) Final Rule for "Occupational Exposure to Blood-Borne Pathogens" (29 CFR 1910.1030) went into effect nationwide on March 6, 1992. Federal OSHA authority extends to all private sector employers with one or more employees, so all church and Christian school employers are covered. All state-level OSHA programs are required to adopt an equivalent standard. In some states, the blood-borne standard requirements have been made an extension of existing health and safety requirements. For instance, in California, the blood-borne pathogen written exposure control plan may be added to a school's existing "Illness and Accident Prevention Program" notebook which was mandated several years ago by CAL/OSHA under CA SB198. Under the OSHA standard, there are substantial fines for employers who fail to protect their employees from exposure to blood-borne pathogens.

## Who Is Covered?

OSHA's rule applies to all persons occupationally exposed to blood or "other potentially infectious material" (OPIM). "Occupationally exposed" means reasonably anticipated skin, eye, mucous membrane, or parenteral (through the skin, such as subcutaneous or intravenous injection) contact with blood or other potentially infectious materials that may result from the performance of the employees' duties. Other potentially infectious materials (OPIM) include human body fluids such as semen, vaginal secretions, any body fluid visibly contaminated with blood and all body fluids in situations where it is difficult or impossible to differentiate between body fluids.

## Exposure Control Plan

The standard requires the employer to develop a written exposure control plan. At a minimum, the exposure control plan must include: 1) the exposure determination for each job classification within your school system; 2) the procedures for evaluating the circumstances surrounding an exposure incident; and 3) the schedule and method for implementing sections of the standard covering the methods of compliance, first-aid reporting procedures, hepatitis B vaccinations, vaccination follow-up, and post-exposure follow-up, communication of hazards to employees through inservice training, and record keeping.

The plan must be reviewed and updated at least annually or whenever new tasks and procedures affect occupational exposure. Copies must be made available to employees and to representatives of OSHA and any similar governmental agency when requested.

## WHO HAS OCCUPATIONAL EXPOSURE?

"Occupational exposure" means reasonably anticipated skin, eye, mucous membrane, or parenteral (pierce, stick, bite, cut, abrasion) contact with blood or "other potentially infectious materials" (OPIM) that may result from the performance of an employee's duties. The exposure determination must be based on the definition of occupational exposure without regard to personal protective clothing and equipment. All job classifications must be reviewed and divided into three groups based on degree of potential exposure. Employees who are required to perform job duties which can result in occupational exposure, even if the individual employee's actual performance of those duties is infrequent, are covered by the standard. Thus, first aid responders such as coaches and playground aides are covered. However, whether or not the employer must provide such employees with pre-exposure hepatitis B vaccinations will depend on whether or not their performance of first aid is a primary or collateral job duty.

OSHA issued a policy statement on July 6, 1992, specifying that while designated first aid providers are covered under the scope of the standard, failure to offer hepatitis B vaccinations to persons who render first aid only as a collateral duty will be considered a "de minimis" violation carrying no penalties, provided that all other requirements of the standard are being met (such as a written exposure plan, annual inservice, the use of standard precautions, documentation of exposure incidents, etc.). OSHA does require that such "collateral" first aid responders who are exposed to blood or OPIM be offered the hepatitis B vaccination series within twenty-four hours of post-exposure.

The First Group is made up of job classifications in which all employees within a classification are designated as responsible for rendering first aid or medical assistance as part of their primary job duties. In this case it is not necessary to list specific work tasks because this group is made up according to "job classifications." This group must have the inservice training and be offered the pre-exposure hepatitis B vaccination series. Examples of job classifications that may be appropriate to include in this group are: school nurses and aides, coaches, and P.E. teachers.

The Second Group includes those classifications in which some of the employees have occupational exposure. Here, specific tasks and procedures causing occupational exposure must be listed with each individual job classification. Employees who administer first aid as a collateral duty to their routine work assignments make up the second group. They must receive the annual inservice training. Post-exposure vaccination must be made available to first aid providers who have rendered assistance in any situation involving the presence of blood or OPIM regardless of whether or not a specific "exposure incident," as defined by the standard, has occurred. It would appear that most school employees such as classroom teachers and aides, administrators, custodians, food service workers, and bus drivers would be covered in this second group.

The OSHA standard does not apply to job classifications in the Third Group. Very few employees' job classifications would fall into this group in a typical school setting. Perhaps the bookkeeper in an adjacent office to the main office of a large school might be an example since that person would not be in contact with students. Even though employees who have these job classifications are not required by the standard to participate in the annual inservice training or be offered the pre-exposure hepatitis B vaccination series, it is simply good management to require the training for all employees. An employee from this group could always end up finding himself/herself in the position of being a "good Samaritan" first aid provider who should be knowledgeable of good health practices.

Since many ACSI member schools do not have a school nurse on duty, administrators may want to review whether it is good policy to continue the common practice of everyone on staff having the "duty to respond" to minor first aid incidents. This automatically puts many employee job classifications in the first group mentioned above. It may be more cost effective (an immunization series may run as high as $150 or more per person), and it may also reduce the number of potentially-exposed employees, if the school rewrites some job descriptions so that certain employees are designated "first aid providers" and then offers this reduced number of individuals the vaccination series and provides them additional training in first aid, CPR, and accident/exposure reporting procedures. More than one person per shift and per building should have that designation with all students needing first aid being channeled by other employees to those with the increased training and personal protection. Individuals other than teachers may be designated "first aid providers." School secretaries seem to perform this function in many schools.

## Communicating Hazards to Employees

Starting June 4, 1992, each occupationally-exposed employee from both the first and second groups must be given information and training. These must be provided at no cost to the employee, during working hours, and at least once a year thereafter. The inservice training must be provided at initial employment before assignment to the job or when existing employee tasks are modified or new tasks are assigned that involve occupational exposure to blood-borne pathogens. Vaccinations must be offered to all employees in Group I job classifications within ten days of starting a job.

If your school employees have not had the inservice training yet, schedule it as soon as possible. Then schedule the annual inservice for back-to-school staff orientation each fall. A health care professional (such as a doctor or local public health official) may provide the training or it may be provided by an appropriate video. The regulations require the training to be "interactive" between the presenter and the audience at each year's inservice so that employee questions will be answered. Therefore, if the training is provided by video, a knowledgeable person, such as a health care professional, must be made available at its conclusion to answer those questions. Perhaps it could be prearranged so that a health care professional utilizing a speaker telephone may answer questions while the staff is gathered at the end of the video presentation.

Training must be in a language and at a comprehension level that the employees understand. It must contain at a minimum the following elements:
- How to obtain a copy of the regulatory text and an explanation of its contents;
- Information on the epidemiology and symptoms of blood-borne diseases;
- Ways in which blood-borne pathogens are transmitted;
- Explanation of the exposure control plan and how to obtain a copy;
- Information on how to recognize tasks that might result in occupational exposure;
- Explanation of the use and limitations of work practice and engineering controls, and personal protective equipment;
- Information on the basis of selection, types, proper use, location, removal handling, decontamination, and disposal of personal protective equipment;

- Information on hepatitis B vaccination such as safety, benefits, efficacy, methods of administration, and availability;
- Information on who to contact and what to do in an emergency including HIV/HBV exposure;
- Information on how to report an exposure incident and on the post-exposure evaluation and follow-up;
- Information on warning labels and signs, where applicable, and color-coding; and
- Question and answer session on any aspect of the training by a health care professional.

Cost-effective ways to help meet this communication requirement are listed in the resources section at the end of this article.

## PREVENTATIVE MEASURES

### Hepatitis B Vaccination

An employer must make the hepatitis B vaccine and vaccination series available to all employees in the First Group and all other employees who have occupational exposure. A post-exposure evaluation and follow-up must also be provided. The vaccine and vaccinations, as well as all medical evaluations and follow-up, must be made available at no cost to the employee, must be provided at a reasonable time and place, and must be performed by or under the supervision of a licensed physician. Employees who decline the vaccination must sign a declination form. The employee may request and obtain the vaccination at a later date and at no cost if he or she continues to be exposed.

The hepatitis B vaccine and vaccination series must be offered within ten working days of initial assignment to employees who have occupational exposure to blood or other potentially infectious materials unless: 1) the employee has previously received the complete vaccination series; 2) antibody testing reveals that the employee is immune; or 3) medical reasons prevent taking the vaccinations. The vaccine is given in three doses over a six-month period. According to one source, 85% to 97% of those vaccinated develop protection against hepatitis B.

Hepatitis B vaccine has been available for many years. Recently, the Centers for Disease Control and Prevention and the American Academy of Pediatrics recommended immunization series beginning in infancy.

## Standard Precautions

"Standard precautions" is the name that the Center for Disease Control and Prevention uses to describe a very aggressive plan that treats all blood and certain body fluids as a source of contamination and infection.

The training mentioned above must also include emphasis on the fact that the use of "standard precautions" on the job is not optional. Employees must know that for their own protection there will be a series of progressive disciplinary steps culminating in dismissal for refusal to follow standard precautions.

## Engineering and Work Practice Controls

Engineering and work practice controls go together. They are the primary methods used to prevent occupational transmission of HBV and HIV. Engineering controls reduce employee exposure in the workplace by either removing or isolating the hazard or isolating the worker from exposure. An example would be the use of a plastic resuscitation device for CPR to avoid mouth-to-mouth contact. The device should be a part of a school's first aid kit. Other examples include the mandatory use of plastic liners in waste paper baskets where Kleenex™ or other disposable items that are bloody may be discarded, and making infectious disease kits (described later) available for each employee. If your school has a school nurse, a "sharps" container should be available for needles and other sharp, disposable items.

Proper work practice controls alter the manner in which a task is performed. This includes such things as requiring hand washing, wearing vinyl gloves, and using an appropriate cleaning solution when cleaning up hazardous materials. Another example would be requiring employees to use a dust pan and brush, cardboard, or tongs to clean up broken glass instead of using their hands.

## Personal Protective Equipment (PPE)

PPE also must be used if occupational exposure remains after instituting engineering and work practice controls, or if those controls are not feasible. PPE includes, but is not limited to, gloves, gowns, laboratory coats, masks, and eye protection. The equipment is considered appropriate only if it does not permit blood or other potentially infectious materials (OPIM) to pass through or reach employees' work clothes, street clothes, undergarments, skin, eyes, mouth, or other mucous membranes under normal conditions of use.

Under the standard, employers must provide, make accessible, and require the use of personal protective equipment at no cost to the employee. Personal protective equipment must also be provided in appropriate sizes. Employers must ensure that PPE is properly used, cleaned, laundered, repaired or replaced as needed, or discarded.

PPE must be removed before leaving the work area or after it becomes contaminated. It must be placed in appropriately designated areas or containers when being stored, washed, decontaminated, or discarded.

Appropriate gloves must be worn when handling or touching contaminated items or surfaces. Be careful not to overlook the custodial staff regarding the required use of gloves in this instance. Never wash or decontaminate disposable gloves for reuse. Utility gloves (Playtex™ type gloves) may be decontaminated for reuse if their integrity is not compromised. Discard utility gloves when they show signs of cracking, peeling, tearing, puncturing, or deteriorating.

Schools should make up "Infectious Disease Kits" for each employee to have in his/her work area. They can be made by filling a Zip-Loc™ bag with a pair of disposable vinyl gloves, a foil packet with a disinfectant towelette, two or three 4" x 4" gauze pads for blood absorption, and one to two Band-aids™. When faced with exposure to blood or other potentially infectious material (OPIM), the employee dons the gloves, cares for the incident, carefully places contaminated items back into the bag, removes the gloves by grasping the top uncontaminated portion and rolls them up inside out as they are removed, places them also into the bag, seals the bag, and then disposes of it in a plastic-lined wastepaper can. The employee is then supposed to immediately wash any contaminated surfaces such as countertops or floors with a disinfectant solution, and personally wash with soap and running water. New kits should readily be available from the school office.

## HOUSEKEEPING

Under the standard, each place of employment must be kept clean and sanitary. To do this, the employer must develop and implement a cleaning schedule that includes appropriate methods of decontamination and tasks or procedures to be performed. This written schedule must be based on the location within the facility, the type of surfaces to be cleaned, the type of contamination present, and the tasks or procedures to be performed.

The employer must ensure that all equipment and environment and work surfaces that have been contaminated with blood or OPIM are disinfected and cleaned immediately. Use a disinfectant approved by the EPA (rated as anti-TB) or a 1:10 solution of household liquid chlorine bleach and water made up fresh daily to ensure proper strength. This can be accomplished by adding 2 cups of bleach to a gallon of water. Allow the chlorine bleach solution to cover the spill for at least ten minutes before wiping it up so it can be properly disinfected. Then a person wearing gloves should remove the bleach-treated spill with disposable wipes. The area should then be washed with detergent and water. The wipes and gloves should be discarded into a plastic bag.

A weaker chlorine bleach solution may be used for routine disinfection of school furniture, counters, and other surfaces. Follow directions on the chlorine bleach bottle.

## LABELING OF BIOHAZARDS AND MEDICAL WASTE

Most ACSI member schools do not typically have biohazards or wastes that would be considered "medical waste" under the standards. However, if a school laboratory has vials of human blood present for scientific experimentation, contact OSHA or your local public health officials for further information regarding required biohazard labeling and disposal regulations.

**NOTE: Feces, urine, nasal secretions, sputum, sweat, tears, or vomitus need not be treated as biohazardous waste unless they contain visible blood. Potentially infectious, soiled feminine sanitary napkins, soiled facial tissues, etc., are not considered a biohazardous waste under OSHA's rules. When handling such waste, employees should wear personal protective equipment such as gloves and wash hands afterwards with soap and running water. Disposal of such items should be into plastic-lined waste containers to prevent further employee contact with the contents.**

## WHAT TO DO IF AN EXPOSURE INCIDENT OCCURS

An "exposure incident" means a specific eye, mouth, and other mucous membrane, non-intact skin, or parenteral (pierce, stick, bite, cut, abrasion of the skin) contact with blood or other potentially infectious material (OPIM) that results from performance of an employee's duties. If an incident occurs, the employee should immediately wash the body area with soap and water. If splashed in the eyes or other mucous membrane, flush that area with water. The incident should be reported immediately to the school administrator. The OSHA standard requires that post-exposure medical evaluation and follow-up be made available immediately for employees who have had an occupational exposure incident. Document all exposure incidents on the "Record of Blood-Borne Pathogens Exposure Incident and Treatment" form and/or any form required by your workers' compensation carrier.

If the infectivity status of the source individual is unknown, the individual's blood may be tested as soon as feasible after consent is obtained. Request for the consent may come from the employee's attending physician. The exposed employee will be informed of the results of the source individual's testing.

Under the OSHA standard, both individuals have the right to refuse the testing, and such a refusal must not affect the "exposed" employee nor the source employee's future employment at the school or the source student's class enrollment. A person refusing the HIV test may have a blood sample taken and held for up to 90 days. If permission is granted during that time, the testing of the sample may proceed. If the source individual is known to be infected with either HIV or HBV, testing need not be repeated to determine the known infectivity.

During all phases of post-exposure, the confidentiality of the affected employee and the exposure source must be maintained. Fines can be heavy for disclosure.

The individuals involved in the "exposure incident" will be directed to a Health Care Professional (HCP). The HCP will receive from the school:

- A copy of its Blood-Borne Pathogens Exposure Control Plan.
- The job description of the employee as it relates to the exposure incident.
- An incident report that explains the route of exposure and circumstances associated with the exposure, and the source individual's serological status, if known.
- The employee's hepatitis B vaccine status and other relevant medical information for both individuals.

The HCP will:

- Evaluate the exposure incident.
- Arrange for testing of the employee and the source individual for HIV and HBV serological status (if permission was granted).
- Provide counseling.

- Evaluate any reported illness.

The HCP will send a written evaluation to the employer including:

- Documentation that the employee was informed of evaluation results and the need for further follow-up.

- Indication of whether the hepatitis B vaccine was required and if the vaccine was received. All other findings are confidential and are not to be included in the written report.

The school must then send a copy of the HCP's written evaluation, within 15 days of receipt, to the exposed employee including the results of any HIV/HAV/HBV testing conducted. (HAV is hepatitis A.)

Following the initial blood test at time of exposure, seronegative employees may be retested again at six weeks, twelve weeks, and at six-month intervals to determine if transmission has occurred. (Common practice seems to be to retest once at three months according to an Infection Control Doctor at one hospital.) During this period, the employee should follow the recommendations provided by the HCP, the U.S. Public Health Service, or his or her local health department.

## RECORD KEEPING

Employers must preserve and maintain for each employee an accurate record of occupational exposure according to OSHA's rule. The school should use the "Record of Blood-Borne Pathogens Exposure Incident and Treatment" form to document the exposure and offer of medical assistance to the affected employee. Note: Some workers' compensation carriers require a similar form with the same information required. An example would be CAL/OSHA's Form 5020—"Employee's Report of Injury" which schools in that state must use. Check with your carrier if you have questions about whether one or both forms should be filled out.

If that person has not previously had the hepatitis B vaccination series, have the individual fill out the "Authorization to Administer HBV Vaccine" form. If the person refuses the vaccination series, he/she must sign the declination paragraph at the bottom according to OSHA regulation. The "Record of HBV Vaccination" should be given to those taking the series. Use the "Medical Consent for Blood-Borne Pathogens Testing" form for the exposure source.

Medical records must contain the following information:

- Employee's name and social security number.
- Employee's hepatitis B vaccination status, including vaccination dates and any medical records related to the employee's ability to receive vaccinations.
- Results of examinations, medical testing, and post-exposure evaluation and follow-up procedures.
- Health care professional's written opinion.
- A copy of the information provided to the health care professional.

Each of the above-referenced reports must be maintained by the school for the duration of an individual's employment, plus thirty years in accordance with 29 CFR 1910.20.

The OSHA standard also requires employers to maintain and keep accurate training records for three years. A sample training documentation form has also been provided with this article. The records must include the following information:

- Training dates.
- Content or a summary of the training.
- Names and qualifications of trainer(s).
- Names and job titles of trainees.

Upon request, both medical and training records must be made available to OSHA representatives. Training records must also be available to employees. An employee's medical records can be obtained by that employee or anyone having that employee's written consent. If the employer ceases to do business, medical and training records must be transferred to the successor employer. If there is no successor employer, the employer must notify OSHA for specific directions regarding disposition of the records at least three months prior to intended disposal.

## Benefits of Compliance

While the school's response to the blood-borne pathogens problem is mandated by law, the primary motivation should be fulfillment of the scriptural injunction to be "our brother's keeper." Hepatitis B can be a serious, even fatal, infection. Other benefits for compliance include:

- Obedience to federal (and most likely state) laws and regulations.
- Reduction in the potential for workers' compensation claims and therefore lower compensation insurance rates.

- The school's possibly-reduced medical and disability costs due to an understanding of standard precautions and vaccination of potential occupationally exposed individuals.
- The building of employee morale by demonstrating that the school cares about the health and safety of its employees.
- The reduction of liability should an exposure incident occur.

## RECOMMENDATIONS

1. Immediately prepare a written "Blood-Borne Exposure Control Plan" to determine how exposure to body fluids will be handled in your school. This includes preparing a list of all job classifications, tasks, and procedures in which occupational exposure occurs.

2. Immediately purchase a resuscitation device to aid in CPR incidents and add it to the school's first aid kit.

3. Immediately make up or purchase "infectious disease kits" so that every employee will have quick access to disposable vinyl gloves and disinfectant.

4. Offer the free pre-exposure HBV vaccination series to all employees in the First Group who are at risk for HBV infection. Also make the free vaccination series available within 24 hours to any other employees who have had blood exposure incidents while on the job.

5. Develop and maintain records and procedures to handle any exposure incidents that occur and to document and comply with the OSHA regulations.

6. Provide annual "interactive" inservice training for every school employee regarding communicable disease prevention, the blood-borne pathogens standards, and standard precautions. Mandate their usage. Document the training.

7. School boards should develop appropriate, written employee/student "wellness" or contagious disease policies. Avoid calling them AIDS policies. Be aware of confidentiality and non-discrimination requirements mandated by federal and state laws.

8. It is advisable for school officials to continue to watch professional journals and check with other sources (local public health officials or other health-care professionals) for information regarding HIV/HBV transmission and prevention. Both the medical and regulatory information will change as time passes.

## CONTACT OTHER AGENCIES

For additional information regarding your response to OSHA's blood-borne pathogen requirements, contact your closest OSHA office. Other good sources of information include your state or district athletic associations, individuals responsible for infection control at your local hospital, and the American Red Cross. The last group has both pamphlets and a video available.

While numerous articles, policies, and other materials were reviewed for preparation of this article, those listed below were particularly helpful and were quoted from extensively in the above article:

Occupational Exposure to Blood-Borne Pathogens, U.S. Department of Labor, Occupational Safety and Health Administration (OSHA 3127), 1992.

Policy materials prepared by the Office of Catholic Schools, Diocese of Arlington, VA, 1992.

Control Program for Occupational Exposure to Blood-Borne Pathogens, LeGrand Union Elementary School District, Merced County, CA.

"OSHA Requires Employers to Give Hepatitis B Immunization and Protection to First Aiders," Dr. Susan Aronson, *Exchange*, November 1992, pp. 55-56.

Memo prepared by Dr. Kim Robert Clark, Redlands, CA, for the CA Department of Education dated March 17, 1993.

Letter from John Howard, Chief, Division of Occupational Safety and Health, State of California, to Santa Barbara County Education Office, dated October 20, 1992.

This article was reviewed for accuracy of basic content by Kelly Howard, Area Manager, CAL/OSHA Consultation Service, Santa Fe Springs, CA; Dr. Kim Robert Clark, CA State University–San Bernardino, lecturer with a doctorate in Public Health; and Dr. Sharon LaHaise-Lewis, Director of Infection Control for Pomona Valley Hospital Medical Center, Pomona, CA.

Reprinted by permission of The Association of Christian Schools International, P.O. Box 35097, Colorado Springs, CO 80935-3509. ACSI is a nonprofit ministry providing services to evangelical Christian preschools, K-12 schools, and Christian colleges and universities. 719-528-6906.

Key portions of this article have been highlighted by the Disciplemaking Ministries Office at Christian Publications, Inc.

NOTE: This article was written ten years ago, therefore some of the information and resources may be dated. The Disciplemaking Ministries Office of The Christian and Missionary Alliance recommends that you review the excerpt from "Clarification of the Standard on Occupational Exposure to Bloodborne Pathogens, 29 CFR 1910.1030," which is located in Appendix M. (For the full article go to <http://www.osha.gov/> and search for CPL 2-2.69.)

For additional information check out the following Web sites:

- www.cdc.gov—Centers for Disease Control and Prevention
- www.osha.gov—Occupational Safety and Health Administration
- www.acsi.org—Association of Christian Schools International

appendix

The guidance that follows relates to specific provisions of 29 CFR 1910.1030 and is provided to assist compliance officers in conducting inspections where the standard may be applicable:

A. Scope and Application - 29 CFR 1910.1030(a). This paragraph defines the range of employees covered by the standard.

1. Since there is no population that is risk free for HIV, HBV or other bloodborne disease infection, any employee who has occupational exposure to blood or other potentially infectious material will be included within the scope of this standard.

2. Although a list is included below of a number of job classifications that may be associated with tasks that have occupational exposure to blood and other potentially infectious materials, *the scope of this standard is not limited to employees in these jobs*. The hazard of exposure to infectious materials affects employees in many types of employment and is not restricted to the healthcare industry. At the same time, *employees in the following jobs are not automatically covered unless they have the potential for occupational exposure*:

   Physicians, physicians' assistants, nurses, nurse practitioners, and other healthcare employees in clinics and physicians' offices; employees of clinical and diagnostic laboratories; housekeepers in healthcare and other facilities; personnel in hospital laundries or commercial laundries that service healthcare or public safety institutions; tissue bank personnel; employees in blood banks and plasma centers who collect, trans-

port, and test blood; freestanding clinic employees (e.g., hemodialysis clinics, urgent care clinics, health maintenance organization (HMO) clinics, and family planning clinics); employees in clinics in industrial, educational, and correctional facilities (e.g., those who collect blood, and clean and dress wounds); employees designated to provide emergency first aid; dentists, dental hygienists, dental assistants and dental laboratory technicians; staff of institutions for the developmentally disabled; hospice employees; home healthcare workers; staff of nursing homes and long-term care facilities; employees of funeral homes and mortuaries; HIV and HBV research laboratory and production facility workers; employees handling regulated waste; custodial workers required to clean up contaminated sharps or spills of blood or OPIM; medical equipment service and repair personnel; emergency medical technicians, paramedics, and other emergency medical service providers; fire fighters, law enforcement personnel, and correctional officers (employees in the private sector, or the Federal Government, or a state or local government in a state that has an OSHA-approved state plan); maintenance workers, such as plumbers, in healthcare facilities and employees of substance abuse clinics.

3. INSPECTION GUIDELINES. The scope paragraph of this standard states that it "applies to all occupational exposure to blood or other potentially infectious materials as defined by paragraph (b)." The compliance officer must take careful note of the definition of "occupational exposure" in paragraph (b) in determining if an employee is covered by this standard.

   a. *Part-time, temporary, and healthcare workers known as "per diem" employees are covered by this standard.*

   b. OSHA jurisdiction extends only to employees in the workplace. It does not extend to students if they are not also considered employees; to state, county, or municipal employees; to healthcare professionals who are sole practitioners or partners, or to the self-employed. However, the 26 OSHA-approved state plans must protect state and local government workers under an "at least as effective" state standard.

   c. If an employee is trained in first aid and identified by the employer as responsible for rendering medical assistance *as part of his/her job duties*, that employee is covered by the standard. See the citation policy for paragraph *(f)(2)* of the standard below regarding designated first aid providers, who administer first aid as a *collateral duty* to their routine work assignments. An employee who routinely provides first aid to fellow employees with the knowledge of the employer may also fall, de facto, under this designation even if the employer has not officially designated this employee as a first aid provider.

d. Exposure to bloodborne pathogens in *shipyard operations* is covered under 29 CFR 1915.1030, which states that its requirements are identical to those in 29 CFR 1910.1030.

e. *Other Industries*: The bloodborne pathogens standard *does not* apply to the construction, agriculture, marine terminal and longshoring industries. OSHA has not, however, stated that these industries are free from the hazards of bloodborne pathogens. For industries not covered by the bloodborne pathogens standard, Section 5(a)(1) of the OSH Act provides that "each employer shall furnish to each of his employees employment and a place of employment which is free from recognized hazards that are causing or are likely to cause death or serious physical harm to his employees." The General Duty Clause should not be used to cite for violations of the bloodborne pathogens rule, but may be used to cite for failure to provide a workplace free from exposure to bloodborne pathogens. Section 5(a)(1) citations must meet the requirements outlined in the FIRM, OSHA Instruction CPL 2.103, Chapter III. Failure to implement all or any part of *29 CFR 1910.1030* should not be, in itself, the basis for a citation. Accordingly, *29 CFR 1910.1030* should not be specifically referenced in a citation.

B. Definitions - 29 CFR 1910.1030(b). The following provides further clarifications of some definitions found in this paragraph:

1. *"Blood"*: The term "human blood components" includes plasma, platelets, and serosanguineous fluids (e.g., exudates from wounds). Also included are medications derived from blood, such as immune globulins, albumin, and factors 8 and 9.

2. *"Bloodborne Pathogens"*: While HBV and HIV are specifically identified in the standard, *the term includes any pathogenic microorganism* that is present in human blood or OPIM and can infect and cause disease in persons who are exposed to blood containing the pathogen. *Pathogenic microorganisms can also cause diseases such as hepatitis C, malaria, syphilis, babesiosis, brucellosis, leptospirosis, arboviral infections, relapsing fever,*

*Creutzfeldt-Jakob disease, adult T-cell leukemia/lymphoma (caused by HTLV-I), HTLV-I associated myelopathy, diseases associated with HTLV-II, and viral hemorrhagic fever.*

NOTE: According to the Centers for Disease Control and Prevention (CDC), hepatitis C virus (HCV) infection is the most common chronic bloodborne infection in the United States. (MMWR: Recommendations for Prevention and Control of Hepatitis C Virus (HCV) Infection and HCV-Related Chronic Disease, October 16, 1998/Vol.47/No. RR-19.)

HCV is a viral infection of the liver that is transmitted primarily by exposure to blood. Currently there is no vaccine effective against HCV. See discussion of paragraph *(f)(3)* below.

3. *"Exposure Incident"*: In this definition, "non-intact skin" includes skin with dermatitis, hangnails, cuts, abrasions, chafing, acne, etc.

4. *"Engineering controls"*: means controls that isolate or remove the bloodborne pathogens hazard from the workplace. Examples include safer medical devices, such as sharps with engineered sharps injury protection (SESIPs) and needleless systems. These two terms were further defined in the revision to 1910.1030 mandated by the Needlestick Safety and Prevention Act.

5. *"Needleless Systems"*: means a device that does not use needles for: (1) the collection of bodily fluids or withdrawal of body fluids after initial venous or arterial access is established; (2) the administration of medication or fluids; or (3) any other procedure involving the potential for occupational exposure to bloodborne pathogens due to percutaneous injuries from contaminated sharps. "Needleless Systems" provide an alternative to needles for the specified procedures, thereby reducing the risk of percutaneous injury involving contaminated sharps. Examples of needleless systems include, but are not limited to, intravenous medication delivery systems that administer medication or fluids through a catheter port or connector site using a blunt cannula or other non-needle connection, and jet injection systems that deliver subcutaneous or intramuscular injections of liquid medication through the skin without use of a needle.

6. *"Occupational Exposure"*: The term "reasonably anticipated contact" includes the potential for contact as well as actual contact with blood or OPIM. Lack of history of

blood exposures among designated first aid personnel of a particular manufacturing site, for instance, does not preclude coverage. "Reasonably anticipated contact" includes, among others, contact with blood or OPIM (including regulated waste) as well as incidents of needlesticks. For example, a compliance officer may document incidents in which an employee observes a contaminated needle on a bed or contacts other regulated waste in order to substantiate "occupational exposure."

NOTE: This definition does not cover "Good Samaritan" acts (i.e., voluntarily aiding someone in one's place of employment) that result in exposure to blood or other potentially infectious materials from voluntarily assisting a fellow employee, although OSHA encourages employers to offer follow-up procedures to these employees in such cases.

7. *"Other Potentially Infectious Materials"* (OPIM): Coverage under this definition also extends to blood and tissues of experimental animals that are infected with HIV or HBV.

8. *"Parenteral"*: This definition includes human bites that break the skin, which are most likely to occur in violent situations such as may be encountered by prison and law enforcement personnel and in emergency rooms or psychiatric wards.

9. *"Sharps with Engineered Sharps Injury Protections (SESIPs)"* are defined as "a non-needle sharp or a needle device used for withdrawing body fluids, accessing a vein or artery, or administering medications or other fluids, with a built-in safety feature or mechanism that effectively reduces the risk of an exposure incident." This term encompasses a broad array of devices that make injury involving a contaminated sharp less likely. They include, but are not limited to: syringes with guards or sliding sheaths that shield the attached needle after use; needles that retract into a syringe after use; shielded or retracting catheters used to access the bloodstream for intravenous administration of medication or fluids; intravenous medication delivery systems that administer medication or fluids through a catheter port or connector site using a needle that is housed in a protective covering, blunt suture needles; and plastic (instead of glass) capillary tubes.

*This directive provides guidance for enforcement of the Bloodborne Pathogens Standard. The agency's application of this policy in any particular matter will, however, depend upon all relevant circumstances. For purposes of providing information and guidance, this directive also restates, clarifies, or ex-*

*plains the provisions of the standard. OSHA's restatement, clarification or explanation of the requirements of the standard does not amend the standard or create new legal duties, obligations or defenses.*

# appendix

## CHURCH ACTIVITY REPORT FORM

_____

*Church/Organization Name*

I would like to take _____ on the following activity:

*Student Name*

This activity will take place on _____ from _____

to _____ .

The other adult(s) who will assist me is/are:

_____

_____

   I will make sure each child has both a parental consent and a medical release form for this activity. I will also not transport more individuals in any vehicle than is legally allowed according to the passenger rating of the vehicle.

_____   _____

*Approved by Appropriate Ministry Leader*     *Signature*

                                    _____

                                         *Date*

SAFE

PLACE

139

# CHURCH ACTIVITY REPORT FORM

_____
_Church/Organization Name_

I would like to take _____ on the following activity:
_Student Name_

_____

This activity will take place on _____ from _____

to _____ .

The other adult(s) who will assist me is/are:

_____

_____

   I will make sure each child has both a parental consent and a medical release form for this activity. I will also not transport more individuals in any vehicle than is legally allowed according to the passenger rating of the vehicle.

_____          _____
_Approved by Appropriate Ministry Leader_                    _Signature_

                                                      _____
_Date_

# appendix

## PARENTAL CONSENT STATEMENT FORM

_____

*Name of Church/Organization*

I hereby consent to let my child, _____ ,

*Student Name*

participate in the following event: _____ .

   It is understood that every precaution will be taken for the safety and well-being of my child, but in the event of accident or sickness, _____ ,

*Church/Organization Name*

its staff and its volunteers are hereby released from any liability.


Signature: _____ Date: _____

Printed Name: _____

Phone: (     ) _____

Address: _____

_____

SAFE
PLACE

# PARENTAL CONSENT STATEMENT FORM

_____

(Name of Church/Organization)

I hereby consent to let my child, _____ ,

*Student Name*

participate in the following event: _____ .

It is understood that every precaution will be taken for the safety and well-being of my

child, but in the event of accident or sickness, _____ ,

*Church/Organization Name*

its staff and its volunteers are hereby released from any liability.


Signature: _____ Date: _____

Printed Name: _____

Phone:  ( _____ ) _____

Address: _____

_____

# appendix P

## MEDICAL RELEASE FORM

_____

*Name of Church/Organization*

Student's Name: _____ D.O.B.: _____

Address: _____ Phone: ( ) _____

_____

_____

Parents'/Guardians' Names: _____

Address (if different from child's): _____

_____

_____

Insurance Company: _____ Policy #: _____

1. Is your child allergic to:

    _____ bee sting     _____ pollens     _____ other drugs _____

    _____ hay, straw     _____ penicillin     _____ other _____

2. Does your child have any life-threatening allergies? ___ Yes ___ No If yes, to what?

_____

_____

SAFE
PLACE

3. Is your child bringing any medication with him/her? ____ Yes ____ No

   If yes, please list and state dosage:

   _____

   _____

   PLEASE NOTE: Medication should be in its original prescription bottle/package, which should have administration instructions and the child's name clearly indicated.

4. Does your child have any physical, emotional, mental or behavioral concerns or limitations

   that our staff should be aware of? ____ Yes ____ No   If yes, please explain:

   _____

   _____

5. Has your child ever had:

   ____ seizures ____ asthma ____ diabetes

   ____ homesickness ____ heart disease ____ other _____

6. Date of last tetanus shot: _____

   In the case of medical emergency, I understand that hospital policy requires parental permission before treatment. I hereby give my permission to a representative of: _____ Church to administer medication as identified above (see #3) and to secure proper medical treatment.

   *Parents will be notified immediately of any medical emergency.*

   Signature of Parent/Guardian: _____ Date: _____

   Emergency Phone: ( ____ ) _____

   Person to contact if parent/guardian cannot be reached: _____

   Relationship: _____ Phone: ( ____ ) _____

# Classroom
# MANNERS

1. Be kind to one another.

2. Pay attention and listen.

3. Follow instructions.

4. Talk one at a time.

5. Keep hands and feet to yourself.

## CONSENT FOR USE OF
## PHOTOGRAPHS ON WEB SITE

This form is to be completed in ink by any applicant for a volunteer position within/ involving: _____

*Church/Organization Name*

I hereby authorize and give full consent to _____

*Church/Organization Name*

to use on their Web site all photographs in which I/my child appear(s) while involved in the ministries of _____ . _____

*Church/Organization Name*          *Church/Organization Name*

may transfer, use or cause to be used, these photographs on its Web site.

I am the parent and/or guardian of: _____
*(Please list all children*
*under your care.)*          _____

          _____

☐ I hereby approve the foregoing and consent to the use of photographs subject to the terms mentioned above. I affirm that I have the legal right to issue such consent.

☐ I hereby do not authorize or grant consent for the use of such photographs.

Signature: _____ Date: _____

*Parent/Guardian*

Witnessed by: _____ Date: _____

# RECOGNIZING SIGNS OF ABUSE

1. Unexplained bruises, burns, fractures or abrasions (often in various stages of healing).
2. Consistent lack of supervision.
3. Consistent hunger, inappropriate dress, poor hygiene or unattended medical needs.
4. Extremes of aggression or withdrawal.
5. Moves with discomfort and shies away from physical contact.
6. Wears inappropriate clothing for the weather in order to cover body.
7. Withdrawn, depressed, listless.
8. Torn, stained or bloody underwear.
9. Irritation of the mouth, genital or anal area.
10. Difficulty sitting or walking.
11. Inappropriate sex play, acting out seductiveness or promiscuity.
12. Sudden changes in school performance, appetite or perceived self-worth.

Abuse or neglect need not have occurred for a student to be in need of protection. It is not necessary to wait until a student has been harmed to intervene. When abuse or neglect can be reasonably anticipated and there are reasonable grounds to believe a student is in need of protection, the necessity of reporting applies. If you have questions about a specific incident, an anonymous phone call can be placed to the Department of Health and Human Services or your local Child Protective Services (CPS) agency to clarify whether or not the given situation constitutes a reportable offense.[1] To maintain anonymity be sure to use a public phone or a private phone that blocks outgoing phone numbers.

## ENDNOTE

1. You can call Childhelp's National Child Abuse Hotline at 1-800-4-A-CHILD (800-422-4453) TDD: 1-800-2-A-CHILD to get the reporting number for your state. Childhelp USA is a nonprofit agency which can provide reporting numbers, and has Hotline counselors who can provide referrals.

# appendix **T**

## SUSPECTED ABUSE REPORT FORM

Date: _____

Name of child/individual: _____ Age: _____

Address: _____ Phone: ( ___ ) _____

_____

_____

Name of parent or caretaker: _____

Name of person filing report: _____

Name of person receiving report: _____

Nature of suspected abuse (physical, sexual, emotional, neglect): _____

_____

_____

_____

Indications of suspected abuse (including facts, physical signs and course of events where necessary): _____

_____

_____

_____

SAFE PLACE

Action taken (including date and time): _____

_____

_____

_____

The above information will serve as a guide and will be necessary if a formal report is filed with the police or appropriate government agency. All information received is to be kept *strictly confidential*.

Signed: _____     Signed: _____

*Person Reporting*                              *Pastor or Designated Authority*

# appendix U

## SUSPECTED ABUSE
## FOLLOW-UP REPORT FORM

Date: _____

Name of child/individual: _____ Age: _____

Address: _____ Phone: ( ) _____

_____

_____

Name of parent or caretaker: _____

Name of person who filed initial report: _____

Name of person receiving report: _____

Conclusions: _____

_____

_____

_____

Action taken (including date and time): _____

_____

_____

_____

The previous information will serve as a guide and will be necessary if a formal report is filed with the police or appropriate government agency. All information received is to be kept *strictly confidential*.

Signed: _____

*Pastor or Designated Authority*